Sunderland
Crawford
William 1
Shields
Russ Hill 22/8/03
Carter
MONTGOMERY
marshall
mccarthy.
Stuart, J

B. Uniting 6/07
Bungay SMR
Heffernan
BALE 8/08
23/64
WALSH, J
Abel Tasman 3/11
AM

THE BENNY
HILL STORY

THE BENNY HILL STORY

JOHN SMITH

with foreword by

BOB MONKHOUSE

ISIS
LARGE PRINT
MAINSTREAM SERIES
Oxford, England
Santa Barbara, California

Copyright © 1988 John Smith
Foreword copyright © 1988 Bob Monkhouse

First published in Great Britain 1988 by
W. H. Allen & Co Plc, 44 Hill Street, London
W1X 8LB

First published in the U.S.A. 1989 by
St. Martin's Press

Published in Large Print 1989 by
Clio Press, 55 St. Thomas' Street, Oxford OX1
1JG, by arrangement with W. H. Allen & Co Plc and
St. Martin's Press

British Library Cataloguing in Publication Data
Smith, John
The Benny Hill story
1. Comedy. Hill, Benny
I. Title
791'.092'4
ISBN 1-85089-301-2

Printed and bound by
Hartnolls Ltd, Bodmin, Cornwall
Cover designed by CGS Studios, Cheltenham

CONTENTS

FOREWORD

by Bob Monkhouse

It was Guy Fawkes Night in 1947 and just as our stage director Bryan Montagu introduced me to the slender young man with thick fair hair, a banger exploded outside in the street. The introduction sounded like 'BenkerPOP'!

'I'm sorry,' I said, 'I haven't got your name.'

'I should hope not,' said the young man, 'I'm not finished with it meself yet.'

Now it wasn't what he said that made the entire cast of our show burst into laughter. It was, as with every great comedian, all in the way he said it.

A week later we presented our intimate revue at the 20th Century Theatre, Notting Hill Gate — two performances only, a showcase of young hopefuls determined to catch the eye of the agents and producers we were assured would be in the audience. I made four appearances and the young man made two — a monologue called 'Sensation on Sunday' and just before the finale, a spot on his own described in the programme as 'Ribbing the *Hipps* ... Bennie Hill.' I can still remember every word of that act. For every laugh I failed to get, 'Bennie' got a dozen.

It seems odd to me now that Benny began as a version of himself. By that I mean he followed in the tradition of front cloth comedians like Ted Ray and Tommy Trinder, a slick patter merchant whose exertion of personality in the theatre was a larger and louder repetition of what you might expect offstage in the pub or at a party.

Yet even then you could detect the assumption of a role. The real man was elsewhere, shyly observing what effect his comic persona was having on us all. Benny was no party clown. The performer in the spotlight was his invention, not the true joker but the joker's messenger.

Even in his early scripts Benny was beginning to hide himself in characters, creations that would later dominate his entire range of productions. Demonstrating what a garrison theatre concert party was like he would become the opening two-girl chorus, he became the dreadful concert party baritone, the third-rate impressionist doing Peter Lorre and Charles Laughton, and the best of his very first eccentrics, a shy Austrian comedian named Toto.

By the time Benny had completed his Toto routine with a crazy Austrian song which he said was called 'Ich Liebe Dich', 'or in English, I Love Richard', his 1951 audience was quite literally hysterical. Written down, it might have seemed flimsy humour. But it was all Benny needed to produce a score or more of facial tics, suggestive smiles, cunning winks, and preposterous word-manglings. Even then he had the answer to his performing needs — matching the simplest words to the funniest characteristics.

Some young comedians tell me that Benny's universal appeal bewilders them. I think they've arrived a little late on the scene. There's well over forty years of rich comedy experience and unerring instinct behind every move that he makes. Those years inform Benny's masterly comic touch so that his art conceals art. Inexperienced eyes and ears and tastes may not be so quickly attuned to the deceptive ease that conceals the complexity of great drawing, great jazz or great cuisine. When Benny throws the camera a double take, it's as perfect as a Pavarotti top note.

Let those who would learn about what makes a comic superstar read this book. Find out what lies behind the image of the world's most famous comedian, because that's what Benny Hill now is. If the answer to why he is can be found anywhere, it's here in these pages. As for the rest of us who just love him, it's a real pleasure to get to know him a little better.

Bob Monkhouse

ACKNOWLEDGMENTS

Many people, from Southampton to San Francisco, helped me piece together *The Benny Hill Story*. My special thanks to: Rosemary Berry, Jeff Blyth, Max Bygraves, Stewart Dickson, Dudley Freeman, Kay Gardella, Annie Jones, Dennis Kirkland, Marvin Kitman, Mrs Ivy Lillywhite, Bob Monkhouse, Mrs Alice Moore, Madame Bettina Olivier, Gavin Petrie, Mick Rhind, Jack Seaton, Don Taffner, Bill Taylor, Reg Varney.

John Smith
London
June 1988

For June and Kevin

CHAPTER ONE

Horse Laughs

It was high noon when Wyatt Earp rode into Dodge City.

Eyes half closed against the blinding mid-day sun he spurred his cantering horse through the mean and dusty streets of the Kansas cowboy town. His strong right hand hovered menacingly over the six gun slung low on his hip.

This was frontier territory, where men were mean as coyotes and wouldn't think twice about putting a bullet in your back.

Well, he'd faced some pretty tough hombres since he first pinned a tin star on his jet-black coat and swore to uphold the law as a US Marshal. Boot Hill was full of wild west gunslingers who'd tried to out-draw him and never lived to tell the tale.

Dodge City was Wyatt Earp's town, and anyone who thought otherwise was likely to end up as just another notch on his Colt .45.

Why, he could still remember the day when Jesse James and his gang rode in from Kansas City looking for trouble, and …

'Hey, Alfie, get a bloody move on. You're late again!'

The strident shout shattered the Marshal's reverie, jerking him back to reality.

Perched high on the seat of a milk delivery cart, young Alfie Hill peered down at the furious upturned face of the company supervisor who bellowed up at him from pavement level.

'Come on, lad, you haven't got all day. Shift yourself!'

With a shrug and a sigh, Alfie clutched the reins of the cart and shivered as he set out through the chill of the pre-dawn darkness.

Daydreams of Dodge City and Wyatt Earp vanished amid the more mundane surroundings of suburban Eastleigh, a quiet commuter town on the fringes of Southampton in Hampshire.

Still, the horse was real enough, even if it was only a friendly little grey horse called Daisy who plodded protestingly between the shafts of the brightly painted cart. Bottles of milk rattling clamorously and sending tinkling echoes through the deserted streets, Daisy broke gratefully into a canter as she reached the brow of Station Hill and clip-clopped down the incline with Alfie Hill yodelling encouragement from beneath the brim of his jaunty peaked cap.

Such moments were fondly stored away in the memory of the white-coated roundsman whose vivid imagination could turn suburban Southampton into the hostile badlands of America's wild west. More than 30 years on, these frontier fantasies would provide the material for a Top Ten comedy record which had the whole of Britain chuckling as they listened to the saga of Ernie, The Fastest Milkman In The West.

For the make-believe Wyatt Earp was an aspiring amateur entertainer who was to find fame as one of the best-known comedians in the world — Benny Hill.

Almost half a century later, Benny's fondest memories still revolve around the days he spent delivering milk to the housewives of Eastleigh. 'It was one of the happiest times of my life,' he recalls. 'Even now it gives me a nostalgic thrill to think of Daisy charging down the little streets, her hooves thud-thudding and the bottles setting up a fine merry jingle.'

There seems to be something more than mere nostalgia which encourages Benny Hill to continually savour these links with the past. He clings to his roots with the dedication of a man who is still not quite sure whether he should ever have left them.

His phenomenal world-wide success has made him a millionaire several times over. But unlike other entertainers who have achieved superstar status he is seldom to be found jetting across the Atlantic on Concorde or entertaining lavishly at some country mansion with a house full of beautiful people and a garage full of Rolls-Royces.

Such frippery appeals not at all to the roly-poly comedian who still insists on washing his own drip-dry shirts and who hand writes all his correspondence on the kind of notepaper that looks as though it has been hurriedly torn from a school exercise book.

The house where he was brought up in Westrow Gardens, Southampton, is still crowded with memories of his mother and father, who died in the 1970s. And it is to this modest, semi-detached home near the Southampton Football Club ground that Benny frequently returns, as if seeking some kind of sanctuary from the relentless razzle-dazzle of show business.

The Hill family had moved to Westrow Gardens from Bridge Road in Southampton, where they were living when Benny was born on 21 January, 1924. They already had one son, Leonard, who had been born several years earlier.

The newcomer was named after his father — Alfred Hawthorn Hill (it would be some 25 years later that he would abandon the first name of Alfie and adopt the name of Benny because he thought it had a snappier ring to it).

Benny's father had been born into a show business family. His own Dad had performed with Bertram Mills' Circus, and at the age of 16 young Alfred had run away from home to join the circus himself. He worked at almost everything, putting up tents, cleaning out cages, hosing down the elephants and even tackling high wire stunts. Sometimes, in more joyous moments, he would make an appearance as a clown.

It gave Alfred Hill Sr a taste for showmanship which never left him. One of his favourite tricks was to amuse Benny and the rest of the family by walking upstairs on his hands.

'He loved to dress me up as a clown,' remembers Benny. 'One of my earliest memories is of my Mum and Dad making me a clown suit out of an old pair of pyjamas and shaping an old hat for me by steaming it and pushing a broom handle into it. I'd do a little clown act in the living room.'

Any hopes that Benny's father had of finding fame beneath the Big Top faded when World War One broke out and he enlisted in the army. After the war he put his entertainment ambitions behind him and settled for a less glamorous life as a commercial traveller, selling surgical appliances. Later he was appointed manager of a surgical goods store in Canal Walk, Southampton.

He was married to Helen Cave, whom he had met when she was a clerk at the Toogoods rolling mills. Although Alfred had a good, steady job — an enviable position amid the economic uncertainties of the 1920s and '30s — he had to be careful with his cash. 'The fact that I've never really enjoyed spending money has something to do with my upbringing,' suggests Benny. 'We were a very frugal family who, without being mean, always counted the pennies.

'To this day I'll think twice about taking a taxi if I know there is a bus or tube train going in the same direction.'

Benny Hill adored his Dad, who adopted a military bearing complete with trim moustache, bowler hat and neatly rolled umbrella. He had been taken prisoner by the Germans during the war, and his favourite party piece was to describe in graphic detail how he had managed to escape — a story which never ceased to enthral Benny, who insisted on passing on the tale in similar dramatic detail to increasingly sceptical schoolmates.

5

The Hill family called Mr Hill 'The Captain'. Says Benny: 'He had a larger than life personality, very much in command. He'd never wait until you had finished speaking if he had something to say.'

While a youngster at Shirley Primary School in Southampton, Benny would catch a bus every Saturday to take his father's lunch to the surgical appliance store in Canal Walk, the food kept warm between two dinner plates. To this day he can still recall the smell of a big leather armchair in the shop and the aroma from the cigars smoked by his father's boss.

The lunch eaten, father and son would play cards. Young Benny almost always won, though he never did discover whether or not this was due to his youthful skill or the paternal benevolence of The Captain.

Sometimes, when his Dad could get the time off, Alfred Sr and Alfred Jr would go fishing on Hythe pier. Theirs was a close relationship, which causes Benny to look back with great affection on his childhood. And this despite the fact that Benny's school chums sometimes sought to embarrass him by drawing attention to the somewhat sensitive nature of certain areas of trade conducted in Mr Hill's surgical shop.

'Hilly's Dad sells French letters,' was the cry that taunted Alf Jr.

Benny got on well with his elder brother, Leonard, even if they did stage spirited pillow fights in the back bedroom of the house in Westrow Gardens.

The two youngsters were allowed to keep a variety of pets which included, at one time or another, a tortoise, a parrot, a cat, a dog and even a goat, which was tethered on the lawn.

It was while he was still at Shirley School that young Benny made his stage debut, a memorable if inauspicious introduction to the world of entertainment. He was nine years old when he appeared in a school production of Alice in Wonderland, with a label round his neck identifying him as 'rabbit'.

'All I had to do was waggle my ears and say ear, ear, ear,' he remembers.

A year later he won a scholarship to Richard Taunton School, a much respected Southampton grammar school where boys were taught to deferentially doff their caps to their elders and betters.

It was while at Taunton's that Benny began to show glimpses of business sense and an aptitude for looking after money which would stand him in good stead in later years. These entrepreneurial skills were inspired by necessity after Benny announced that he would rather like a bike, and his father's response had been: 'Bikes cost money.'

Benny became quite a shrewd little trader, scrabbling through the school dustbins to retrieve gold plated pen-nibs which he sold for cash. Southampton being a seaport, there was always plenty of foreign money around, handed out by generous sailors on shore leave. Benny collected anything from American dimes to German pfennigs, profitably converting them into pounds, shillings and pence.

'I can remember one bit of wheeling and dealing which netted me the princely sum of £2,' says Benny.

'I had a single cigarette card which another boy needed to complete his set. So I sold it to him for a halfpenny. With the halfpenny I bought a battered toy racing car which had cost sixpence when new. I swapped the car for an old model yacht, painted the yacht and exchanged it for a cricket bat. I passed on the bat in return for a chemistry set and traded this for a magic lantern with slides. I swapped the magic lantern for a model railway, which I sold to a second-hand shop for two pounds.'

People began to take notice of young Alfie Hill, and he had no objection at all to occasionally being the centre of attraction. 'I was a king-size show-off,' admits Benny. 'At football I played goalkeeper, and when the ball came slowly towards me I used to wait until the last minute and then hurl myself into the mud to make a dramatic save. Parents were watching, and I loved the cheers.'

Art was Benny's favourite subject and his art master, Mr Alan Witney, remembered him as 'a jovial, cheerful lad with a pleasant round face.' The teacher was quite impressed by Alf's artistic efforts. 'I kept a plaster cast he did of a nun,' says Mr Witney. 'It wasn't a great work of art, but I still think it has a poetic quality. He also did paintings which showed imagination.'

Outside of art, school lessons held little attraction for Alfie.

And if the lad's mind didn't always seem to be on his work amid the rigid discipline of Taunton's it was because his imagination had been fired by a far more exciting distraction.

Alfie Hill had fallen under the magic spell of the Music-Hall.

In the pre-war days of the 1930s, live entertainment was enormously popular and a trip to the music-hall to see the likes of 'cheeky chappie' Max Miller was the highlight of the week for thousands of people. Most towns had at least one variety theatre, and many cities had three or four.

The Hills loved the music-hall, and every Wednesday night the entire family would go to either the Palace or the Hippodrome in Southampton, to see artists like Sandy Powell, Wee Georgie Wood and G. H. Elliott.

Quite often the shows were supposedly racy revues with titillating names like *Cheeky Days, Don't Be Saucy, Naughty But Nice* and *Toujours Les Femmes*.

Although such productions were pretty tame by modern standards, they did frequently fill the stage with pretty girls.

But it was always the top of the bill comic who mesmerised Alfie Hill as he sat enraptured in the sixpenny seats, munching chocolates supplied by his grandad.

Up there behind the footlights, grease-painted face slyly acknowledging the laughter and enthusiastic applause, the comic was king.

To the young schoolboy, watching wide-eyed from his seat high up in the 'gods' it seemed the most glamorous and exciting job in the world.

'The comedian was the centre of attraction,' Benny remembers. 'Everyone loved him, laughed at him. And with him there were always the saucy girls, the glamour, the French maids with black stockings, knickers and feather dusters who would stick their bottoms up.

'At the end of every song or dance routine the girls would put their arms around him and kiss him on the cheek. Well, I ask you, I used to think to myself: "This man leads the life of Reilly. That's going to be the life for me one day ...".'

Back home in Westrow Gardens, Alfie couldn't wait to emulate the stand-up comedians who had become his idols. A blanket slung over his shoulder in place of the loud checked jackets much favoured by such performers, he would stand in the front room and lean forward to confidentially deliver jokes about 'the wife' in best Max Miller style.

Mrs Hill, vastly amused by the antics of her small son, made him a large George Robey style hat out of papier mache and he borrowed her lipstick and rouge to give himself the authentic 'made up' look of the professional entertainer.

Alfie was an excellent mimic, and extended his repertoire to include personalities like Louis Armstrong and Jack Buchanan. Sometimes he would sing, with his Dad scraping an accompaniment on a one-string fiddle.

His father encouraged him to take up the guitar, and at the age of 14 Alfie got together with three classmates at a school concert to deliver an impersonation of the Mills Brothers (they called themselves The Hills Brothers). The delighted applause with which the act was received was music to his ears.

'I didn't wear a shirt and I had "beer is best" written in blue ink across my chest,' recalls Benny. 'The audience laughed, and I rather liked that. I was living.'

Despite his growing interest in entertaining, Alfie had found time to develop a keen interest in another hobby — cycling. At the same time he became enthusiastic about the new sport of motorcycle speedway racing, which took place on a track near his home. Ever the dreamer, he would cycle along the loose gravel of an area called The Clump, jamming on the brakes of his bike and skidding sideways in a cloud of dust just like the motorcycle aces he'd seen at the speedway.

But there was less and less time for cycling as he was bitten even deeper by the show business bug. He auditioned for Bobbie's Concert Party, a semi-professional group who played in working men's clubs in the Southampton area.

Despite the youthful looks of Master Hill, they were impressed by the chirpy confidence of the youngster whose speciality spot was a comic impression of a vicar in which he appeared in a back to front collar and large helpings of his mother's makeup and rouge.

'The Young Mothers' Club requires new members,' the 'Rev.' Hill would advise his audience. 'If there are any ladies who would like to become young mothers, please see me after the service.

'We are having an additional font installed at the front of the church, so that in future babies can be baptised at both ends.

'The couple who are getting married on Saturday have asked for a quiet wedding, so I shall be wearing carpet slippers for the ceremony.

'And remember, if any ladies wish to bring eggs for the harvest festival, will they please lay them just inside the entrance.'

At other times the vicar's outfit would be discarded in favour of a smart-looking dinner jacket which Hill

Jr had bought for five shillings in a second-hand shop. The sophisticated routine which went with this man-about-town act earned him the nickname 'The Posh Boy'.

Never the most dedicated of students, Alfie could hardly wait to leave school at the age of 15. Such a premature end to a youngster's education might be looked at askance nowadays. But in pre-war Britain it was not unusual for children to finish their schooling at the age of 13 or 14.

By this time the budding comic had equipped himself with a 'cheekie chappie' checked jacket and a vivid red tie for his stage appearances.

His act included a favourite gag in which he remarked on how cold the weather was, then reached into his pocket to produce a handful of paper 'snowflakes' which he threw over his head in a miniature blizzard.

Young Alfie seemed determined to launch himself on a full-time career in show business. But it seemed a particularly inopportune time for someone so young to tackle the uncertainties of the entertainment profession.

The year was 1939, and Britain was at war with Germany. No one could tell just how things would turn out. His father persuaded Alfie that a good steady job would be preferable to the gamble of a life in show business.

So, reluctantly, Alfie began work as a weighbridge clerk at the Phoenix Coal Company in Southampton. It was not a success. Writing down details about lorry loads of coal proved a somewhat tedious occupation for the teenager whose head still danced with visions of the music-hall comic sharing the spotlight with a bevy of beautiful girls.

Still, there were some compensations in the dreary job which paid just 17s 6d a week. They came in the eye-catching form of a pretty young girl who worked in the same office.

'I fell madly in love with her,' confessed Benny. 'After weeks of trying to pluck up courage, I finally asked her one evening if I could walk her home. To my delight she said Yes.

'But to my dismay she promptly jumped on her bicycle and started to pedal off. I like a challenge, so I still took her home — trotting along beside her and chatting away.

'She lived four miles out of town, and I didn't even get a kiss for my trouble.'

The experience did little to enhance Alfie's disposition to coal office clerking, and he left after only a few weeks.

Show business still beckoned, but Alfie's father still cautioned against it. Mr Hill had a friend at the Palace Theatre in Southampton, and arranged to take Alfie backstage to show him the somewhat tatty and un-glamorous accommodation provided for the perform-ers.

'Show business isn't a Betty Grable film with silken couches and dressing rooms the size of Salisbury Plain,' announced Mr Hill as they looked in at the cramped changing rooms with pockmarked mirrors bordered by naked light bulbs.

His son hardly heard him. He was totally oblivious

to the tawdry surroundings and was gazing in awe at the second string comic dabbing on greasepaint as he prepared to go on.

Stage-struck though he was, the footlights still stayed far away for eager Alfie. His father was still dead-set against a show business future and arranged for Alfie to go along for a job interview with a business contact who was manager of the Woolworth's store in Eastleigh, just outside Southampton. To Mr Hill's delight, Alfie was offered a job as a stockroom clerk.

'Use your head and you can work your way up to £15 a week,' Mr Hill assured him.

Once again Alfie found himself in a job which was both tiresome and unappealing. 'I had to wear a long, brown warehouse coat and check over all the goods,' remembered Benny. 'I couldn't stand all the paper-work involved.

'Quite apart from the clerical work I had to handle all the heavy stuff. I sold lino, shoved and shifted bales of material and humped hundredweight sacks of pea-nuts.'

Again, though, he had found a job with an unex-pected bonus. Alfie and the manager were the only two men on the staff, among about 40 shopgirls. But Alfie's attempts to cut a dash with these alluring young ladies were doomed to failure.

One of his many duties was to clean up after cus-tomers' dogs who had disgraced themselves on the shop floor. 'Day after day I would pray I could sink through the floor when I heard the manager call "Oh, Mr Hill … toilet," shudders Benny. 'Out I would go with my little broom and dustpan.

'Apparently all the different smells on the cosmetics counter were guaranteed to bring out the worst in even the best behaved dogs. Which was doubly unfortunate, as I was in love with a girl called Jean who worked in cosmetics. Nearly every time I met that girl I was on my hands and knees cleaning up the floor beneath her feet.'

'This lovely girl, a really good-looking blonde, came to associate me with the kind of smell they never put in bottles.'

Nevertheless, the girls took a liking to the chirpiness of the cheery stock room clerk who kept them amused with his impersonations and funny voices. They called him 'Sonny Boy', and if Alfie was anxious to surround himself with sweeter smelling aromas than he normally encountered with his dustpan and brush duties, the shop assistants were only too eager to help him out.

'A box full of Californian Poppy perfume arrived with all the bottles broken, and the bottom of the box was swimming in the stuff,' recalled Benny. 'A few of the girls crept up and poured it all over me. No matter how many baths I had, I smelled of Californian Poppy for months.'

Any regard which Alfie might have had for the job in Woolworth's wore off long before the smell of Californian Poppy. He quit after six months and, much to the dismay of his father, signed on as a milkman to drive a horse and cart for the Hann and Son dairy in Eastleigh. Mr Hill Sr thought it a terribly unwise and undignified move, and grumbled to friends that his son had turned his back on a career which could have taken him right to the top in Woolworth's.

But there was something about the freedom and outdoor life of his new job which really appealed to 16-year-old Alfie, and it was a breath of fresh air after his unhappy experience in the coal office and Woolworth's. Because it meant a 5.30 a.m. start, he moved out of the family home and took lodgings with a Mr and Mrs Brown in a road called The Nook in Eastleigh. It was the beginning of one of the happiest periods of his life.

The appearance of smiling Alfie, perched high up on the milk cart, was a tonic for housewives beset by the problems of wartime rationing. 'He was always happy-go-lucky whenever you saw him,' said Mrs Nellie Smirk whose husband, Eddie, was the dairy foreman. 'He'd unload his cart, then come across, cracking jokes and making everyone laugh.'

More than 45 years on, the details of those carefree days with Daisy the horse still remain fresh in Benny's mind. 'My first customer was about a mile and a half out of the town,' he remembers.

'So if the dairy had a horse or mare that hadn't been in the shafts before and was inclined to be frisky, they would give it to me. That's because if the horse wanted to run, you didn't have to worry about traffic and it was more than a mile before I needed to stop.

'Up Station Hill we'd go, and down the other side at a fine pace, bottles rattling away in the back. Then, with a loud "whoa, there!" I'd bring the horse to a halt and leap down to greet my first customer with a cheery Milk-O!'

Alfie Hill had only to slip the reins into his hands for

his imagination to run riot as he set out on his rounds. 'One day I'd be Wyatt Earp, riding into Dodge City,' he explains. 'Or maybe a stage-coach driver, pursued by Indians. When I turned into Market Street, I always felt like a knight on a white charger.'

For many customers the arrival of 'that nice little chap Alfie' was a high spot in their dreary day.

They would make him tea and laugh at his jokes as he sat in their kitchen, munching a piece of the home-made cake which was becoming more and more difficult to produce because of the rationing restrictions on the essential ingredients. 'He'd have us all in stitches,' said Mrs Annie Spreadbury, one of his regulars.

His bosses at the busy dairy, however, were not always so amused. 'He should have finished his round by 1.30 pm but it was always 3.30 before he was through,' sighed dairy inspector Ernest Hewett. 'With all his fooling and pranks, he was always late.'

Alfie kept both workmates and customers amused with impersonations of some of the more colourful characters he met on his round. A favourite was an elderly lady who frequently came to the door minus her false teeth, holding a dish cloth to her mouth to hide her embarrassment. 'The trouble was that speaking through a dish cloth without her teeth in rendered her almost completely incoherent,' observed Benny. 'Making any sense out of her order was one of my hardest jobs.'

For an aspiring comedian on the lookout for characterisations, there were rich pickings on the Eastleigh milk round. With the strictures and shortages of wartime Britain becoming more onerous every day, officialdom had become the target of many a disgruntled family.

'The average housewife appeared to be governed, regulated and intimidated by a mysterious collection of people she described as "they",' said Benny. '"They" were the people who were under some kind of obligation to minister to her needs, and make life smooth and comfortable for her.

'"They" would provide ration books, egg allocation cards and the rest. "They" had to come and repair her kitchen window or see about the smell on the landing.'

When 'they' had failed to come up to expectations, particularly in sensitive areas like egg rationing, it was Benny who took the full brunt of the housewives' ire. Benny did a perfect impersonation of an outraged housewife, arms crossed and face quivering with indignation. It was a huge hit with the lads at the depot who were suffering similar tirades themselves.

His round finally finished, Alfie would frequently pop into one of Eastleigh's two cinemas on Market Street — the Picture House and the Regal. Munching his lunch (cakes and ice-cream, plus sweets from the dwindling stock of Maynard's shop) the young milkman avidly watched films like *Drums Along The Mohawk* with Henry Fonda and Claudette Colbert.

The Regal was his favourite because it had an organist who played a selection of popular tunes before the main feature film.

It was a simple and happy enough existence, but the lure of show business was still with the youthful Alfie. Sometimes he would take the train to the Grand

Theatre in Basingstoke, hanging around the stage door and waylaying some of the lesser-known comedians as they arrived for the first house. 'Fancy a drink after the show?' inquired Alfie.

Sometimes they would accept this invitation from the fresh-faced youngster, and over half of bitter they would tell yarns about life on the road, with amusing stories about life backstage and the perils of theatrical 'digs' and dragon landladies.

Alfie was enthralled, and wouldn't hesitate to confide to them his own entertainment ambitions. One comedy double act invited him backstage to their dressing room, where Alfie did an impromptu comedy routine for them.

'Quite good, son,' they said. 'We might be able to use you. We're going up north for a few weeks, and we'll look you up when we're down this way again.' But they never did come back, and Alf's momentary dream of stardom vanished with them.

When such setbacks threatened to get him down, he would cycle to his favourite spot, a hill overlooking Winchester. The sight of the ancient cathedral city spread out below him somehow blunted the bitter disappointment he felt inside.

His parents, still unhappy about their son earning a living as a 28 shillings a week milkman, were still urging him to get a 'proper job'. He might even have done just that if he hadn't heard about a vacancy in a local concert party which performed in the Eastleigh area. The group were called Ivy Lillywhite and Friends, with Ivy herself on the piano and a lineup which included a drummer, violinist and trumpeter.

Ivy opened the door of her home in Dutton Lane, Eastleigh, one evening to find a chubby-faced teenager standing on the doorstep clutching a guitar. 'My name is Alfie Hill,' he said. 'I play the guitar and sing.'

'I invited him in, and he sang a song for me,' recalls Ivy. 'It wasn't particularly marvellous, but it would certainly help, as one of the group had been called up into the Army.'

Ivy Lillywhite and Friends played mainly at dances and social evenings, and Alfie's contribution was mainly confined to crooner-style renderings of popular songs like 'Begin the Beguine' or 'Just A Little Love, A Little Kiss'.

The only comedy was supplied by the trumpeter who occasionally clowned around with his instrument.

Alfie soon changed that. He persuaded Mrs Lillywhite to let him try a few comedy routines as they toured the district, playing in venues which ranged from Boy Scout huts to working men's clubs. Out came the vicar's outfit, and with it the jokes about baptising at both ends.

'He would practise at my house,' says Mrs Lillywhite, 'dashing in and out of the kitchen with various bits of funny business, constantly asking "what do you think of this?"'

Gradually young Alfie introduced more and more comedy into the shows. 'He was getting better and better, but he didn't always go down well — and you could see that that hurt him.'

The year was 1940, and signs of war were everywhere. Southampton swarmed with men and women in uniform, and the docks had become a target for German night-bombing raids. Adopting the old troupers motto that the show must go on, Alfie and the band hurried through the darkened streets, walking to their numerous engagements with Mrs Lillywhite holding her music case over her head in the hope that it would protect her from falling shrapnel.

It was a hectic time for Alfie. Doubling on guitar and drums for the band (plus nasal-sounding solos on ballads like 'Careless Love'), he often didn't get home from engagements until 2 a.m., leaving him just over three hours' sleep before getting up to start his milk round.

In addition, his cheeky chappie stand-up comedy routine was beginning to earn him a reputation locally. Benny still remembers being paid out by the manager of the Eastleigh Town Hall who told him: 'Believe me, lad, I'm sorry it's only five bob. You were worth every penny of seven and six.'

But it was all getting too much. 'I was burning the candle at both ends,' said Benny. 'I couldn't keep a regular daytime job and carry on in the entertainment business. It had to be one or the other.'

The choice wasn't difficult. He gave in his notice at the dairy, and raised £8 by selling his guitar and drum kit. Then he bought a coach ticket to London and announced to his anguished parents that he was off to seek fame and fortune in the bright lights of the West End.

'I'm not quite sure what I had in mind,' confesses Benny. 'I had a misty idea of a cigar-hazed lunch in a Mayfair hotel, the champagne flowing as some film tycoon signed me up for his latest epic.'

There was a tearful family farewell in Southampton (by now he also had a small sister, Diana). His father, despite misgivings about his son's decision, shook him by the hand and gave him an additional £3.

Wearing a blue serge suit and carrying a brown cardboard suitcase, Alfie Hill strode confidently along Westrow Gardens and headed for the coach station and the bus to London.

He was just 17.

CHAPTER
TWO

London Lights

There was nothing very glamorous about London in the summer of 1941.

The devastated city was still reeling in the aftermath of the Blitz in which it was bombed night after night by about 200 German aircraft. In one single night the enemy dropped 350 tons of bombs, more than they had dropped on Britain in the whole of the First World War.

Alfie Hill knew a bit about air raids. Southampton had also been a frequent target for the German bombers. But the youngster was shocked by the scale of the destruction which met his gaze as the coach from Southampton threaded its way into central London through areas which had taken the full brunt of the bombing.

Whole streets had vanished, rows of houses turned into nothing more than piles of rubble. Buildings gutted by fire stood like burned and blackened skeletons and teams of workmen scurried everywhere shoring up half demolished houses and fencing off huge craters left by 250lb bombs.

Londoners on their way to work picked their way through the debris, and in St James's Park tin helmeted ack-ack gun crews searched the skies for any signs of further attacks. In Hyde Park, air raid wardens and other civil defence workers prepared to be reviewed by Prime Minister Winston Churchill — his way of saying 'well done' for their heroic efforts which had somehow seen the city survive.

Suddenly, amid the desolation, a poster caught Alfie Hill's eye. In big letters it said: 'If it's laughter you're after, Trinder's the name — you lucky people.'

Like everyone else who saw the poster, jutting up jauntily above the rubble-strewn streets, Alfie Hill smiled. It was entertainers like Tommy Trinder who had managed to keep the nation chuckling through even the darkest days.

The posters had been the cockney comedian's own idea, a little gimmick to follow up on his success in a show called *Top Of The World* with the Crazy Gang at the London Palladium.

'You lucky people' was Trinder's catch-phrase. Office boys had adopted it and bellowed it cheerily to workmates as they took round the morning tea.

Catch-phrases were catching on. The entire nation echoed to cries of 'Vereee good, sir', as delivered by Jack Warner in a popular radio programme.

Bumping through the city on the bus from Southampton, Alfie Hill pulled a scrap of paper from his pocket and started working on a few possible catch-phrases for himself. If nothing else it took his mind off the increasing nervousness which was beginning to overtake him as the coach nudged its way to Victoria coach station.

He was alone in London with £11 in his pocket, nowhere to live, no job, no prospects, no friends and no idea how to get started on the stairway to stardom.

What he did have was that week's issue of *The Stage* newspaper, the 'bible' of the entertainment industry. Listed near the front were the London 'calls' which showed where the various performers were currently appearing. Top of the list were Max Miller and Vera Lynn, starring in *Apple Sauce* at the London Palladium.

Despite the war, the London theatre business was booming, having recovered from the first uncertain months of the conflict when the Home Secretary had banned all public entertainment in the metropolitan area because of the threat of air raids. However, theatre programmes still carried warning notices which said: 'Should an air raid warning be received during the performance the audience will be informed from the stage. The warning will not necessarily mean that a raid will take place, and in any case it is not likely to occur for at least five minutes. Those desiring to leave the theatre may do so, but the performance will continue and patrons are advised in their own interests to remain in the building.'

Just below this notice was often to be found an advertisement showing a bearded seaman with his boots off, gratefully massaging his bare feet. The caption underneath read: 'Thank goodness we keep some

TCP on board. It's simply indispensable, say men and women on war service.'

Walking up Whitehall towards Leicester Square, Alfie Hill looked again at the theatre listings in *The Stage*. He was tempted to head straight for the Palladium, bang on the stage door and ask if they could use a good comic. But as their current top-of-the bill, Max Miller, was the best-known comedian in the country the lad from Southampton shrewdly decided that more promising prospects might well be found in less competitive company.

In Charing Cross Road he stopped a passing policeman and asked where he could find the nearest suburban music-hall.

'Brixton Empress would be your best bet, son,' said the kindly copper, directing him towards a bus stop. As the double decker headed for south London, Alfie sat on the top deck and once again consulted the 'calls' in *The Stage*. Heading the bill at the Brixton Empress was Sid Seymour and his Mad Hatters Band, an act which Alfie had seen on one of his music-hall outings in Southampton.

His spirits rose. The Mad Hatters band were a crazy group who got up to all kinds of antics on stage. Surely they'd be able to find room for a young comic who'd had them rolling in the aisles with his funny vicar turn at Eastleigh Town Hall?

Sid Seymour came to the stage door himself, and Alfie was surprised to see that the man who appeared to be a big, bluff north countryman in front of the footlights turned out in the cold light of day to be a somewhat smaller and older gentleman with a twitch.

He listened patiently to Alfie's pleas for a chance with the band, a small spot in the show — anything.

'Sorry, son, there's nothing for you,' he said. 'Have you tried Streatham?'

The Streatham Hill Theatre was featuring a touring revue called *Bring On The Girls*, and Alfie got short shrift from the company manager who took one look at the lad in the blue serge suit and ducked back inside with a swift shake of his head.

Disconsolately dragging his suitcase, and growing more disillusioned by the minute, Alfie decided to try his luck back on the other side of the River Thames. He headed for the Chelsea Palace, where a touring manager called Harry Flockton Forster was running a show for impresario Harry Benet.

There was something about the eager youngster from Hampshire which made an immediate impression with Harry Forster. It may just have been that Alfie Hill was big for his age and not eligible for immediate call-up at a time when shows like the one at the Chelsea Palace were being depleted by artistes being drafted for the armed forces.

Whatever the reason, it was sufficient for Forster to tell the delighted ex-milkman that he thought Harry Benet should see him. He fixed an appointment for Alfie to see the great man in his Soho office the next morning.

'Yippeee!' Alfie shouted his joy to the summer skies as he swaggered through the streets of Chelsea, swinging his suitcase with the nonchalance of a young man firmly headed for fame and fortune.

Well, that was the future taken care of. The more

pressing problems were involved with the present. Where, for instance, was he going to spend the night?

Alfie still had most of his £11 left, but he was reluctant to splash out on lodgings.

Suddenly, a thought came to him. Where did thousands of Londoners spend their nights? Why, in air raid shelters, seeking safety from German bombing raids which by this time had greatly decreased because Hitler needed the Luftwaffe for the invasion of Russia.

Earlier in the day, from the top of a bus, Alfie had spotted some shelters on Streatham Common. So it was there that he headed, bedding down for the night with his suitcase as a pillow.

The next morning he washed and shaved in the gents' toilet at a local Lyons Corner House, then headed for his appointment in Soho. A lifetime later, Benny Hill retains every detail.

'I had recently bought myself a grey pork pie hat with a little orange feather at the side,' he recalls. 'When I went into Harry Benet's office I pushed the hat to the back of my head and sat on his desk. I'd seen James Cagney do it in a gangster film, and I was trying to foster a tough, cheeky wise-cracking image.'

With a confidential wink, Alfie fixed the startled impresario with a confident grin and said: 'I'm a comic. If you want your audiences rolling in the aisles, I'm your man.'

Somehow the showman restrained himself from coming round from behind his desk and throwing the bumptious youngster out into the street by the scruff of his neck. Instead, he guided him to a chair in the poster-lined office and said gently: 'Now sit down, son, and listen.

'No one is going to accept a comedian who doesn't look as though he has started shaving. But you can learn your trade properly, like George Lacey who started with me as a property boy on £2 10s a week. Look at him now.'

Blushing slightly, Alfie nodded his acknowledgement. George Lacey was a household name.

'I'll tell you what I'll do,' offered the impresario. 'I'll give you £3 10s a week, and you will be the assistant stage manager and do small parts as well.'

Apologising profusely for his initial brashness, Alfie gratefully shook Benet's hand and left the office carrying, not wearing, his James Cagney hat with the feather in the band.

By the time Alfie reported for work at the East Ham Palace in London three days later, he had swapped the Streatham air raid shelter for a bed in an East End lodging house where he shared a huge room with Merchant Navy sailors who frequently woke up screaming as they relived the nightmare of sailing through German U-boat packs with the Atlantic convoys.

The show at East Ham Palace was a revue called *Follow The Fun*, starring comedian Hal Bryan. As assistant stage manager, Alfie found himself humping baskets of props and scenery and doing a dozen odd jobs including brewing pots of weak tea to double as 'beer' in sketches featuring the show's several comedians.

In between, one of the cast showed him how to use the professional's 'five and nine' greasepaint and he made his professional stage debut in a patriotic scene at the end of the show in which he was dressed as John Bull with a cushion stuffed up his Union Jack waistcoat, shaking hands with another performer dressed as Uncle Sam.

Young Alfie loved every minute of it, even if the biggest part he was given was only that of a uniformed policeman shouting the order 'Call Mrs Worthington' in a comedy courtroom sketch.

Towards the end of the week he was backstage laying a kitchen table for the next scene when he sensed that something was going wrong on the other side of the curtain where comedian Hal Bryan was supposed to be doing a cross-talk sequence about going out to fetch beer.

'All by myself and nobody about,' wailed the comedian. 'Oh, I wish I had a friend to talk to. Isn't there anybody I can talk to?'

Listening behind the curtain, Alfie realised at once what was wrong. Hal Bryan's straight man, who was supposed to partner him in the sketch, was known for taking a drink or two too many. On this particular night he was too far gone even to make it on stage.

Alfie Hill knew what he had to do, but somehow he couldn't get his legs to function. Heart thumping, and still wearing his stage manager's overall, he forced himself to walk out on stage and deliver the opening line which he had been listening to all week.

'Hello, hello, are you going to it?'

'No, coming from it,' said Hal Bryan, adding with a grateful hiss: 'Thank goodness you've turned up. Now, say: Where can you get any beer round here?'

'Where can you get any beer round here?' As if in a dream, Alfie heard himself repeating the whispered lines.

'There's a pub down the road,' proclaimed Hal Bryan, followed by a whispered: 'Keep going son. Now you say: I'd give anything for a pint.'

Somehow, with Bryan's sotto voce coaching, Alfie stumbled through to the end of the sketch. He left the stage with the applause of the audience ringing in his ears and Hal Bryan firmly gripping him by the arm.

'Here, son, take this,' said the veteran comic, offering him a ten-shilling note. 'You're going to be a trouper.'

The show went out on tour, with Alfie acting as baggage master, loading scenery and props aboard trains bound for provincial towns and cities all over Gt Britain. The theatrical 'digs' where they stayed were often dreadful, and audiences sometimes hard to please — it was rumoured that in Sunderland the audiences were two inches taller than in the rest of the country because they were sitting on their hands.

But Alfie didn't care. At the age of 18 he was a fully fledged 'pro'. An entertainer.

Follow The Fun was followed by another revue called *Send Him Victorious*. Alfie confessed to an occasional fit of the giggles when the entire cast sang a patriotic chorus of Land Of Hope and Glory as many of them were frightened to death of being called up.

When the shows were 'rested' between tours, Alfie earned himself an extra £2 a week acting as a watchman in a hessian warehouse in Southwark. He had to be there 24 hours a day, which suited Alfie as he could sleep on a little truckle bed and save himself money on lodgings.

But he grew so pasty-faced that his workmates began to get worried about him. 'Go on, lad, take a few hours off,' they urged him one night. 'We'll stand in for you.' Still wearing his boiler suit, Alfie headed for the London Palladium where he sat in the dress circle watching Naunton Wayne and Vic Oliver.

Sitting in the darkness of the famous theatre he vowed that one day soon it would be Alfie Hill they'd be applauding up there in the spotlight.

Unfortunately, such ambitious plans were to be interrupted by the demands of His Majesty's Forces. Police turned up at a Cardiff theatre where young Hill — by this time 19 years old — was appearing in another Hal Bryan show. They demanded to know why he hadn't reported for Army service, as ordered.

Brushing aside his protests that he didn't know what they were talking about, the constables took him to Cardiff police station where he was locked in a cell for four nights. Then a military escort arrived to take him to Lincoln barracks where he was put to work scrubbing floors in the detention room.

'I was treated like a criminal until it was all sorted out,' says Benny. Inquiries revealed that Alfie's papers had failed to reach him because of a mix-up in forwarding mail from one theatre to another, a common hazard for performers who were almost constantly on the road.

Not that it made any difference. He was drafted into the Royal Electrical and Mechanical Engineers as a driver mechanic, a period of his life which holds few happy memories. 'I loathed it,' he says. 'Route marches, manoeuvres oh, I did resent it. Half the sergeants were power mad, calling us privates up from the ranks and yelling "You're a dozy little man, what are you" and we had to reply "I'm a dozy little man, sergeant".'

Alfie Hill confessed to being the worst driver mechanic in the British Army, even though he learned to drive almost every type of vehicle, from jeeps to heavy trucks. 'I've never driven a car since,' he reports.

'Every time I see a car I remember the long nights when they'd bring a busted engine in and say: "Fix that by morning."'

'I was five years in the Army and never got a stripe. But I was crafty. I ran dances and things to get me off guard duty.'

By his own account, Private Hill got closest to combat when his unit, the Third Light Ack-Ack Searchlight Battery Workshop, were sent to Dunkirk soon after the D-Day invasion. 'I spent the rest of the war near Dunkirk where we had 7,000 Germans encircled,' he explains. 'They couldn't get out, and we couldn't get in. Every so often we would pop over a few high explosive shells, just to let them know the war was going on.'

Despite his dislike for military life, there was one Army unit which had a great deal of appeal for the young comedian whose show business career was so rudely interrupted by hostilities. This was the army entertainments division, which put on shows for the troops under the name *Stars in Battledress*. These featured performers like Sergeant Charlie Chester, who was later to attain immense popularity with a post-war radio show called *Stand Easy*.

By the time Alfie put in his application for a transfer to the entertainment section, the war had ended and his own unit was stationed in the German town of Osnabrück. Ever the clown, Alfie entertained the local kids at Christmas by parading round the streets dressed as Santa Claus, with a NAAFI ping-pong ball painted red stuck on his nose.

Stars in Battledress seemed in no great hurry to recruit the unknown comic from the REME who assured them in his letter that his act was just the stuff to give the troops. Weeks went by and he heard nothing. There was still no word by the time he was due for leave in London.

The city bore the scars of the German air raids, and landmarks like St Paul's Cathedral were surrounded by huge open bombed sites, whole areas which had been absolutely levelled by the Luftwaffe.

But the Londoners in the streets had a chirpy, almost cocksure air about them. Hitler had done his worst, and they'd taken everything he'd thrown at them and survived. No wonder they whistled their way to work.

Alfie made straight for the Nuffield Centre, off Trafalgar Square, where the *Stars in Battledress* team were headquartered. He had written a few sample scripts, some dialogue which he thought might suit the perky style of 'Cheerful' Charlie Chester. But the Army captain who received him wasn't over-enthusiastic.

'We have plenty of writers,' he said. 'What we need

are performers. Do you do anything?'

Visions of his funny vicar routine rushing through his head, Alfie Hill nodded. 'Er, yes, I do some stand-up stuff,' he said.

'Jolly good,' said the officer. 'Come back tomorrow and we'll take a look at you.'

Wandering through the West End in his khaki uniform, Alfie anxiously turned over in his mind the material which he had performed with Ivy Lillywhite's group in Southampton. The comic vicar was O.K., but he would need something more substantial to impress the entertainment brass hats.

Close by Piccadilly Circus, he came to the Windmill Theatre. Studying the posters outside, Alfie spotted a familiar name: Peter Waring. He was a suave, immaculately dressed comedian whom Alfie had seen perform several times in Southampton and whose smooth style he greatly admired.

Sitting in the crowded stalls of the Windmill, Alfie was delighted to find that the elegant Mr Waring was sophisticated as ever. Wearing impeccable tails, he reeled off a languid monologue peppered with almost laconic throwaway lines.

By the time he faced the panel of auditioning officers at the Nuffield Centre the next morning, Alfie had worked out an equally relaxed monologue, based on a rambling shaggy dog story about a man catching a train from London and studded with snap impressions of everyone involved including the ticket collector.

The officers liked it. Back in Germany three weeks

later, Private Hill's transfer papers came through. He was a Star in Battledress.

Well, not quite. He was given a small part in a musical comedy called *Happy Weekend* which opened with great success at the Opera House in Calais, and then went on tour round military bases in Britain. But the experience he had gained with Hal Bryan's touring revues before he was called up began to show, and when *Happy Weekend* ended he was sent as a solo performer to an Army entertainments pool just outside Hamburg in Germany.

He became compère of a band show, doing 13 spots to introduce numbers by the band and various guest artistes. Audiences seemed to like him, and everything seemed to be going swimmingly until the Major who was second-in-command of the Hamburg unit watched him for the first time in rehearsals.

'That's not funny at all, Hill,' he insisted. 'We can't send you on with routines like that. You'll get the bird.'

Alfie was shattered. It looked as though the Major's decision would mean his leaving the show. But a sergeant called Harry Segal, who had taken quite a shine to the breezy young comic, came to his rescue. 'Stay with the show,' he said. 'We need someone to look after the baggage.'

From wise-cracking compère to case-humping baggage man wasn't exactly the kind of career move that Alfie had in mind. But his luck was in. On the last night of the tour, at the Crown Prince Theatre in Hamburg, several of the acts in the show went down with flu.

Desperate for performers to fill the gaps, Sgt Harry Segal turned to Alfie. 'Get on there and do 10 minutes,' he ordered.

Donning a silk dressing gown and the kind of laid-back approach he'd seen Peter Waring adopt at the Windmill, Alfie strolled on stage to face the packed audience of service men and women.

'I cracked a few gags and they roared with laughter,' he remembers.

Sitting in the front row was the commanding officer of the entertainments unit, Colonel Richard Stone, who had been a stand-up comedian himself before the war. He was quite taken with the confidence of the young comedian he had never seen before, and the next morning phoned the Major who had previously pulled Alfie out of the show.

'Why wasn't Hill on for longer?' demanded Col. Stone. 'Er, I didn't think he was all that funny, sir,' faltered the Major.

'Well, that just shows how much you know about comedy,' stormed Stone. 'In future Hill will compère the entire show. And that's an order.'

For the next year Alfie toured with service shows all over Britain and the Continent, entertaining the troops in France, Belgium and Germany. But it all came to an abrupt end in 1947 when Alfie was demobbed.

Confident that this experience with Army entertainment would open the doors to the big time, he headed for London with his £50 service gratuity in the pocket of his grey striped demob suit.

He found, however, that the streets of London

weren't paved with gold. They were covered with out-of-work comics. The service shows had been the breeding ground for a whole new generation of comedians, including performers like Max Bygraves and Frankie Howerd.

Stars in Battledress was one thing. Stars in Civvy Street was quite another.

CHAPTER
THREE

Uphill and Down

'So, anyway, this sergeant goes up to the officer, and he says ...'

'Yes, thank you very much. Next!'

From somewhere in the darkened stalls, the weary voice floated across the footlights and on to the cramped stage of the Windmill Theatre, halting Alfie Hill in mid-joke.

The young comedian could hardly believe it was happening. He had been on stage for less than a minute, scarcely time to get through a couple of gags, and here was this disembodied voice ending the audition almost before it had started.

'But, I was just ...'

'Next!'

The voice from the darkened stalls, by now sounding slightly impatient, cut across Alfie Hill's attempts to explain that his act had only just begun and that he had much more sparkling material to unfold if only they would give him a few minutes more.

But the Windmill had no time to spare. Waiting in the wings was a queue of aspiring comics, all equally anxious to impress Vivian Van Damm, the tiny theatre's notoriously tough proprietor.

Tucked away in Great Windmill Street, just off Piccadilly Circus, the Windmill Theatre was the target of every ambitious young comedian in the scramble for post-war success.

It had originally been a cinema and was doing only very moderate business as an intimate theatre when, in 1937, Van Damm pulled a master stroke which was to turn the Windmill into one of the best-known venues in the land. He introduced nudes.

Having stayed open throughout the war ('We Never Closed' was its proud boast), the 312-seat theatre was doing tremendous business by the time Alfie Hill turned up for his audition there in 1947.

Van Damm had recruited a stunning collection of beautiful girls who posed almost naked in a series of tableaux. But, by order of the government's Lord Chamberlain's Office, watchdog of public morals, they were not allowed to move. In addition, no 'artificial aids to vision' were permitted in the theatre, so punters who frequently turned up clutching powerful German binoculars — personal spoils from the recently completed Second World War — were temporarily relieved of them at the door.

The star of the show was fan dancer Anita D'Ray, who peeked provocatively from behind a pair of black ostrich feathers while giving the riveted all-male audience the occasional tantalising and fleeting glimpse of bare flesh.

Comedians hired by Van Damm were little more than temporary distractions, a diversion while scenery was changed and the audience scrambled frenziedly over the seats to claim any places vacated in the front rows.

The comics' pay was about £20 a week, and despite the fact that they were surrounded by beautiful girls backstage it was hard work doing six shows a day, six days a week for audiences who had come to ogle nude women and considered comedians an annoying and unnecessary seven-minute interruption.

It was a tough training ground, but it provided an early showcase for a generation of comedians who were to become household names: Tony Hancock, Morecambe and Wise, Harry Secombe, Harry Worth, Dick Emery, Jimmy Edwards and Arthur English.

Alfie Hill, however, was not destined to join the Windmill alumni. His barrack room humour failed to impress Van Damm, who sat unseen in the stalls, and Alfie lasted less than a minute before the dreaded dismissal of 'Next!' was shouted from the shadows.

But the experience taught him a valuable lesson. 'In the army, any gag about officers or NCOs could be depended on to raise a laugh from an audience of soldiers,' he reflected. 'But it was a different kettle of fish when I was demobbed. Civilian audiences wanted more.'

That was a lesson being learned by a whole battery of young comedians, many of them fresh out of the services.

'Because we had all done so well in the forces we

were all bigheaded enough to think we could make a living at it,' suggests Max Bygraves, who also joined the post-war comedy circuit after doing more than 500 shows in the Royal Air Force.

'But it wasn't as easy as we thought.'

The area around Leicester Square and Charing Cross Road in London's West End was dotted not only with theatres but also with the offices of theatrical agents, and it was to this bustling entertainment Mecca that show business 'pro's' flocked in search of work.

Many of the theatrical agencies were little more than a cubbyhole of an office, almost invariably guarded by a hard faced secretary whose main job appeared to be preventing callers from getting anywhere near the agent himself who sat surrounded by old music-hall posters and who seemed to be for ever clinching some major deal over the telephone.

Unknown comics like Alfie Hill, however, seldom got to see the great man himself. More often than not, Alfie would climb a flight of narrow stairs, ring the bell alongside a nameplate which read 'Starlight Theatrical Agency' or something similar and be confronted by the secretary who popped her head out through a hatch to inquire aggressively: 'Yes, what is it?'

'Er, my name is Alfie Hill, I'm a comedian and I thought maybe Mr Ross might fix some bookings for me.'

'Where can we see you work?'

'Well, I'm not working at the moment. That's why I've come.'

'Well, how can we get you work if we can't come

and see your act?'

Then the hatch would slam and Alfie would dejectedly make his way back out into Charing Cross Road, where sooner or later he would be able to relate the experience to sympathetic fellow performers who had all gone through similar encounters.

The Express Dairy in Charing Cross Road was a favourite meeting place for out-of-work entertainers and it was here, lingering over cups of tea which they could ill afford, that Alfie and his new-found friends discussed the worthless nature of ignorant agents who wouldn't know star material if you hit them over the head with it.

It was around this time that Alfie Hill decided to change his name. He had toyed with the idea of calling himself Alf Hill, but decided that sounded too much like a cockney comic. Still hankering after the sophisticated approach of his idol Peter Waring, he thought Leslie or Benny might conjure up the desired image American comedian Jack Benny was another of his idols.

In the end it was Benny which he chose. 'It has a touch of the one gold tooth and lounge suit about it, don't you think?' he inquired, trying it out on friends.

As if to officially confirm his new identity, he splashed out a precious £2 on having some visiting cards printed. Exit Alfie Hill — enter Benny Hill (Comedian).

Britain was anxious to cheer itself up after the gloom of the wartime years, and music-hall was booming. A contract with one of the major theatrical chains, par-

ticularly Moss Empires, could keep an artiste in con-
tinuous work for more than a year, playing the numerous theatres in London such as the Finsbury Park
Empire and Wood Green Empire and then doing a
week of twice-nightly performances at Moss theatres
scattered throughout the provinces.

But the erstwhile Stars in Battledress found it difficult to make the breakthrough into this profitable circuit. Instead, they had to be content with bookings at
public houses and London working men's clubs such
as the Tottenham Liberal and Radical Club.

The White Swan at Walthamstow and the Tithe
Barn near Harrow were two pubs where Benny Hill
delivered his cheekie chappie routine, a stand-up spot
of quickfire patter sprinkled with carefully nurtured
'ad-libs' guaranteed to make the most of even the most
unexpected situation.

Such was the informal atmosphere of these venues
that Benny would sometimes spot a mother breast-
feeding her baby in the audience.

'After you, Georgie,' suggested Benny, grinning
saucily at the baby.

'You'll be lucky,' responded the Mum.

'Ooh, I hope so,' sighed Benny, eyes raised in mock
ecstasy.

Customers returning from the lavatory would be
buttonholed from the stage by Benny, who demanded: 'Could you hear us in there?'

'No.'

'Well, we could hear YOU.'

It was a hard slog making audiences laugh in such
smoky, crowded and rowdy surroundings. But it was

also invaluable experience, and Benny looks back on it with a certain amount of fondness. 'Some of those places were an education,' he observes. 'I did the lot, even such "A" class venues as Tilbury Docks.'

Carefully eking out the £50 gratuity with which he had left the Army, young Benny travelled to engagements by bus or tube, often having to walk miles when a late spot at a club meant that public transport had shut down by the time he had finished. On the meagre fees he was being paid, he couldn't afford a taxi.

Max Bygraves still has a letter he sent to the Harlesden Social Club in 1949, apologising for the fact that he would be unable to fulfil a planned engagement there and suggesting: 'There is a fellow around named Benny Hill who can do the date. He is very good.' The fee: £2.50.

By comparison with other places that Benny played, Harlesden was a big earner.

Comedian Bob Monkhouse remembers meeting Benny in Belotti's coffee shop in Shaftesbury Avenue, another favoured rendezvous for young performers eager to swap gossip and steer each other in the direction of helpful agents or possible engagements.

'Benny told me about a place called the Ridgeway Club in Hammersmith,' says Bob. 'Then he put three fingers up to the lapel of his coat and said: "This is what they pay."'

Noting the three outstretched fingers, Bob was delighted. A payment of £3 for a night's work was good money at a time when £1 was nearer the norm.

'It was a terrible club, and I suppose I had just the act to match it,' says modest Monkhouse. 'Anyway, at the end the entertainments secretary came over and said: "It was three we were going to pay, wasn't it?'"

Bob nodded, holding out his hand and expecting to receive three crisp £1 notes. To his dismay, he was handed three half crowns. Monkhouse had completely misinterpreted the three finger lapel sign which he later learned was part of a form of tic-tac used by theatrical agents who didn't like to be overheard discussing money matters.

The fact that Benny was prepared to work for so little was some indication of just how much of a struggle he was experiencing in trying to get himself established.

Bob Monkhouse, at that time still in the R.A.F., had first met him in 1947 when they appeared together in a revue called *Spotlight* at the 20th Century Theatre in Notting Hill Gate, West London.

It was a tiny theatre, popular as a showcase for aspiring young amateurs and professionals. If nothing else it was somewhere agents could come and see them work.

Monkhouse noticed right away that this mischievous-faced Benny Hill had a real professional touch about him. For one thing, he had a bright red tongue. It was obvious to Bob, who knew about such things, that Benny was using Gordon Moore's Cosmetic Toothpaste, a trick employed by music-hall comedians to give their tongue additional colour and prevent it looking yellow under the spotlight.

The toothpaste was intended to tint gums crimson, thus making teeth look brighter. But the pro's found it just as useful for tinting the tongue.

Benny (who was mortified to find his brand new name spelt Bennie in the programme) did an act called 'Ribbing the Hipps' which was supposed to be a satire on music-hall comedians (the 'Hipps' being the Hippodrome-style theatres which staged variety). To this end he wore a bright red tie, enabling him at an early stage to look down and rear back in mock alarm, confiding: 'Phew, for a moment there I thought my tongue was hanging out.'

'Benny did his variety act, but it had to have a touch of satire to fit in with the revue format of the show,' Monkhouse remembers.

'He got huge laughs. Half the audience thought it was funny because it WAS funny, and the other half thought it was funny because it was satirical.

'But it wasn't really satirical. It was Benny at his early best. Already he had assembled his apparatus of physical tricks, the intimate glance, the lowering of the lids, the little smirk. He was the best thing in the show.'

Although the *Spotlight* revue played to only small audiences in the tiny 20th Century Theatre, the success of his act prompted Benny to audition again at the Windmill Theatre.

With Vivian Van Damm once more watching from the stalls, Benny did a quickfire routine which was a skit on a variety bill in which Benny adopted various guises, ending up as the star of the show, Issy Connor — a combination of Jewish comedian Issy Bonn and Irish tenor Cavan O'Connor.

It was good, but not good enough. This time he lasted two and a half minutes before the now familiar

'Next!' ended the audition.

Disappointed and dispirited, Benny sat alone at a table in the back of the Express Dairy in Charing Cross Road and took stock of his situation. He was sharing a flat in Queensway with three girl dancers called Lynne, Dorothy and Hazel. His share of the rent was £2.25, which entitled him to use the gas ring in the cramped kitchen for cooking.

The £50 with which he had left the Army had by now dwindled to almost nothing.

His dreams of stardom shattered by the harsh realities of show business, he packed his few belongings in his battered cardboard suitcase and walked to Victoria coach station, where he bought a bus ticket to Southampton.

He wasn't quite sure what he'd do when he got there. Certainly the thought of going back on the milk round didn't seem a very attractive prospect. Nor, indeed, did the idea of facing friends and family and admitting that his bid for fame and fortune had ended in failure.

To add to his gloomy frame of mind, mechanical problems meant a delay of two hours before the coach left for Southampton.

With time to kill, Benny was wandering by the Biograph cinema in Victoria and was interested to see they were showing a film starring a performer he much admired — American comedian Danny Kaye. Thinking it would fill in the time until the coach left, Benny hurried inside and was just in time for the start of the movie, *Wonder Man*.

Danny Kaye was in top form, fooling his way

through a story which was a colourful mixture of drama and comedy, set against a roisterous night club background. The versatile Mr Kaye played a mild-mannered student who is persuaded by the ghost of his dead twin to avenge his murder.

Sitting in the back row, Benny began to imagine himself in the Danny Kaye part, clowning around with hard-faced gangsters and being befriended by beautiful women.

'Suddenly — or was it slowly — there dawned on me the idea that I could do as well as Danny Kaye,' Benny recalled later. 'Here was this world-famous Hollywood star, with the gorgeous Virginia Mayo in his arms, wearing a diaphanous nightie (Virginia, not Danny) and I COULD DO AS WELL AS THAT.'

Benny (after unsuccessfully demanding a refund) tore up the coach ticket to Southampton and made his way back to the flat. Anything Danny Kaye could do, he could do better.

The problem was that this was no Hollywood fantasy in which our hero, in his darkest hour, is suddenly seized by inspiration and turns tragedy into triumph before strolling off into the sunset with a beautiful girl on his arm.

The stairway to stardom still began within the humble confines of the Express Dairy cafe or the salt beef bars around Carnaby Street where performers hung about in the hope of buttonholing an agent or two. On a good day you might even bump into the great Lew and Leslie Grade, snatching a quick sandwich on a brief break from conducting high-flying business at their London Management headquarters in nearby Regent Street.

And the steady work still lay in the working men's clubs, like the Edmonton Trades Club, who still paid £1 a concert. By 'doubling up' and playing two clubs on a Saturday night, Benny could make as much as £5 in a good week.

This often meant travelling across town by bus, with no time to take off his make-up between engagements. The sight of a young man with his face plastered with 'five and nine' greasepaint and a tongue coloured bright red by Gordon Moore's cosmetic toothpaste often attracted curious glances from his fellow passengers.

Sometimes he felt obliged to provide some kind of explanation and would chirpily volunteer: 'Oy, Oy, actor!' before burying his head in the evening paper to avoid the continuing stares.

A pub called the Captain's Cabin in Lower Regent Street had become something of a 'labour exchange' for comedians seeking work, a place where Benny could compare notes and trade gags with other aspiring funny-men like Max Bygraves, Norman Wisdom and Tommy Cooper.

Lunch was invariably taken at the nearby Old English Eating House which served a substantial steak and kidney pudding for 2s. 6d.

'The clubs where people like Benny and myself played were scattered all over London — Plumstead, Dagenham, Harlesden,' recalls Max Bygraves. 'You were always on the run, working out how you could get to these bookings by bus or tube.

'Yet it was a lovely feeling. It was a great atmosphere, and you were never bored. You were achieving something.'

As the months went by, Benny Hill was certainly achieving something. From the working men's clubs he had graduated to the cabaret circuit, doing Masonic dinners at a heady three guineas a night.

He had also acquired an agent — Richard Stone, his old colonel from the Army entertainments unit who had spotted Benny's talent during the *Stars in Battledress* tour in Germany. Demobbed from the Army, Colonel Stone had abandoned the idea of continuing his career as a stand-up comic and instead had opted to open a theatrical agency in London. Benny was one of his first signings.

Constantly trying out new material, all of which he wrote himself, Benny's stage act had become much slicker and more professional. He had carefully studied the styles of American comedians like Danny Kaye, Dick Shawn and Danny Thomas, and would often take the germ of an idea from their routines and re-work it in a style which suited his own inventive approach.

'He developed an astonishingly wide range of "bits" very rapidly,' says Bob Monkhouse. 'Having been stationed in Germany during the war, he spoke a kind of German doggerel which he used to good effect.

'One of his spots was to pull a bowler hat down so that his ears bent double, and he would come on stage as a German lecturer. He had a lot of bits like that, where he took a series of gags which seemed to be unrelated and combined them in these routines.'

But Benny still lacked the 'big break' about which

all performers dream. It came in 1948, when impresario Hedley Claxton was looking for a 'feed' for his star comedian, Reg Varney, in the Hedley Claxton *Gay Times* show at The Lido, Cliftonville, in Kent.

There was a rush of applicants for the job, but a series of auditions finally whittled down the list to Benny and one other young comic with a likeable line in slightly zany humour. Benny was chosen, and the other disappointed comedian was left to pursue stardom through some other channel. His name was Peter Sellers.

Before setting up for the summer season in Cliftonville, the *Gay Times* shows toured the provinces. Besides playing straight man to Reg Varney, Benny was also given his own solo spot on the bill.

Benny's solo act wasn't a huge success, and some clue as to why that was so comes from Reg Varney, the talented comedian who went on to become a television star in series like *The Rag Trade* and *On The Buses*.

'Benny did stand-up patter, a bit similar to Bob Monkhouse,' recalls Reg. 'But he hated doing his stand-up spot.

'I remember once we were in digs together while playing the Alexandra Gardens in Weymouth. Benny was obviously worried about his solo spot. He came to me and said: "God, it's frightening. I can't go on. My mouth dries up, and I can't spit a tanner."'

By coincidence, Reg Varney had been suffering similar anxieties. Being principal comic in such a popular show was a heavy responsibility, and the chirpy cockney comedian had been unable to sleep because he was constantly worrying about how well the production was doing.

Reg had sought the help of a therapist who had given him lessons in how to relax, a routine which involved tensing and relaxing each part of the body in turn.

Says Reg: 'I told Benny about it and he said "Cor, blimey, I'll try that tonight." I saw him at breakfast the next morning and he said: "No, Reg, it didn't work, I started to try it, but I was so tired I turned over and went to sleep!"'

While Benny's stand-up comedy may not have been a runaway hit in the *Gay Times* show, his partnership with Reg Varney worked splendidly.

'As a "feed", Benny was brilliant,' enthused Reg. 'We became very close, and in fact we became so good that he only had to look at me and he KNEW just what was required when we were on stage together.

'He would sense that I wanted him to feed me with something, or I would look in his eyes and I knew there was something he had in mind. It was uncanny, the understanding we had between us.

'I remember one night at The Lido when the back curtain stuck and they couldn't go on with a big production scene. Benny had just finished his solo spot when Hedley Claxton came rushing in in a great panic and said: "Quick, get out there, do something!"

'I didn't know what we were going to do, we had no act prepared or anything. But Benny went on, twiddling his hands together as he always used to, and he went into this routine about how he had been sent on to explain that the big waterfall scene should have been next, only there was a slight snag.

'Then I ran on stage, all indignant, and said: "Just a minute, I'm the compère here." And so it started. I was dodging about behind his back, pointing to his teeth and hair and miming the word "false" to the audience.

'Benny was ad-libbing like mad, and somehow or other we did a whole impromptu act together. It couldn't have been better if we had rehearsed it.'

It was Benny who helped Reg Varney to create one of his most famous sketches, a tennis routine called 'What The Deuce'. The two comics were sitting in deckchairs in the garden of Varney's home near Ramsgate when the idea for the sketch suddenly came to Reg, and he got Benny to scribble down the outline on the back of a packet of Players cigarettes.

It involved Reg dressing up as a 1920s-style woman tennis player, complete with frilly drawers and a bandeau round his forehead.

The idea was that he was a shy little girl who had joined a tennis club because she couldn't get a boy friend, and Benny played the tennis instructor.

Some sample lines:

'I must say I like your dress.'

'Thank you. It's the A-look.'

'The A-look?'

'Yes. Everyone stops and says: Hey, look!'

Benny and Reg may have been enthusiastic about this new sketch, but Hedley Claxton certainly wasn't. 'He took one look at it and declared it a disaster, and said he couldn't let it go on,' Reg Varney remembers. 'But I told him it HAD to go on, because we had nothing else new.'

Claxton was so certain that the sketch would be a gigantic flop that he shut himself in his office while it was on, ashamed to share the embarrassment which he felt sure would follow.

To his amazement, he heard the audience rocking with laughter as Reg and Benny romped through the routine. 'Benny was absolutely magnificent,' reflects Reg. 'The way he made use of his face, his eyes, was terrific.'

Benny did three seasons with the *Gay Times* show, and his amazing rapport with Reg Varney seemed to have secured a very bright future for the up-and-coming Mr Hill.

The two of them in 1950 were invited to join a touring version of a show called *Sky High*, which had been a big success at the London Palladium with Jimmy Edwards as the star. Reg was signed to take over from Edwards in the road show, and Benny was included as Varney's straight man.

The producers of *Sky High*, George and Alfred Black, didn't need a solo comedy spot from Benny. They were reluctant to risk using a relatively unknown comic in such a costly and successful production.

But Benny pleaded with them, and reluctantly they allotted him a seven-minute spot in the first half.

'I know it's awful to say, but Benny's act was always the weak link in that show,' says Varney.

Disaster struck when the show reached Sunderland Empire, a notorious 'graveyard' for southern comics. 'I was in my dressing room while Benny was on, and I heard the audience clapping,' says Reg. My first thought was: 'Christ, he's going well.' Then I realised.

They were giving him the slow handclap. I'd never heard it before. It was awful.

'Benny came off stage white-faced, and was terribly sick in the dressing room sink. Oh God, I cried for him.'

The show's London management rushed a representative up to Sunderland and ordered Benny to drop his solo spot immediately. They were quite happy for him to continue as 'feed' to Reg Varney. But his seven minutes were chopped.

'Benny told them he didn't want to end up just being my feed,' Reg remembers. 'That was understandable. He was too good for that. He had this great gift for different voices and accents. A German, a Scotsman, anything like that and he was outstanding.'

Benny stayed with the show another week while another straight man was recruited to take his place. Reg Varney tried to change his mind about leaving, but Benny was adamant.

Richard Stone, Benny's agent, was furious at this development. 'Don't be a fool,' Stone told him. 'You're on a good, steady wicket getting £35 a week. Reg Varney is going to be a big star at the Palladium and there is a future for you in being his straight man. Look at Jerry Desmonde.' (Jerry Desmonde was the 'feed' for the immensely popular comedian, Sid Field.)

'But I don't want to be a straight man, I want to be a comedian,' said Benny, plaintively.

'Well, I can't book you as such, and I don't know anyone who can,' raged the agent.

Reg Varney was close to tears when he and Benny

shook hands after the curtain came down on the young Southampton comic's final appearance in *Sky High*.

'What are you going to do, Benny?' inquired Reg.

Benny gave one of his familiar, shy smiles. 'Don't worry about me,' he said. 'I'll think of something.'

CHAPTER
FOUR

On Camera

A small crowd had gathered on the pavement outside the electrical shop in west London.

They pressed forward against the window of the store, jostling for position to get a good view of the television set with a 12-inch screen which stood on a display stand, flickering away in black and white.

The show they were watching was *What's My Line*, a panel game in which a team of celebrities had to guess the trade or profession of the guests who 'signed in' with a brief mime which was of little or no use when the contestant turned out to be something obscure like 'a sagger maker's bottom knocker'.

Elbowing his way to the front of the crowd, Benny Hill stood transfixed by the small screen, smiling at the ill-tempered antics of a panellist called Gilbert Harding whose grumpiness and impatience with some of the more frustrating contestants was rapidly turning him into the nation's Mr Nasty.

Benny took in every detail of the irascible Mr Harding, mentally noting his bristling, military style moustache, rasping voice and aggressive stare through heavy, horn-rimmed glasses. The germ of an idea had begun to form at the back of Benny's brain, an idea in which he could well make use of the blustering mannerisms of grumpy Gilbert.

It was not unusual to see little knots of people gathered round demonstration TV sets in shop windows in 1951. Radio was still Britain's main entertainment medium and television was something of a novelty.

There were only about a million TV sets in the country, mainly grouped round the major cities because many areas didn't yet have facilities to receive television signals from the transmitters in London.

Not that those without TV sets were really missing much. The programmes were spectacularly unadventurous, leaning heavily towards instructional interludes like Fred Streeter's gardening hints or cookery lessons with the bearded chef, Philip Harben.

Music-hall performers were very wary of this new medium, whose listings were confined to a four-page section at the back of the *Radio Times* which still gave priority to radio and obviously considered television little more than a newfangled novelty which did not deserve to be taken seriously.

Variety agents in particular considered TV taboo, strongly advising their clients against getting involved with it. Live entertainment was still hugely popular in the early '50s, and even a performer with only one act could comfortably tour the provincial music-halls happy in the knowledge that his return appearances at any one theatre would be so well spaced out that there was little danger of his routine becoming too familiar from over-exposure.

Television was an obvious threat to such a cosy and lucrative arrangement. Many leading comedians only had one main routine, and even though the number of homes with TV sets was comparatively small it would be suicidal to throw away a lifetime's material for the sake of a brief appearance in front of the cameras.

Speciality acts such as jugglers, magicians and acrobats were even more cautious, for if it was difficult for comedians to come up with new scripts for television it was almost impossible for visual acts to re-work their routines in a way which would give their performances a fresh look on TV where they would inevitably be playing to audiences who had already seen them at some time or another on the variety circuit.

The immediate result was that the few variety shows screened by the BBC (who held the monopoly on TV broadcasting) were bland and boring, relying heavily on lack-lustre continental cabaret artistes.

Benny Hill, who couldn't afford his own TV set, had nevertheless been able to see enough of this new entertainment to begin thinking that it might just hold some possibilities for a performer like himself.

Six weeks had slipped by since his disastrous experience at the Sunderland Empire, an episode which had seriously dented his self-confidence.

If nothing else, it had made him face up to the fact that his heart really wasn't in the endless grind of twice-nightly variety as a stand-up comic. Years later, looking back on the time he spent touring in the provinces, he recalled: 'It was wonderful when the audiences cheered. But the next time you opened they could be stone cold.

'The band leader in the orchestra pit would shake his head despairingly. And after the show the manager would just tut-tut at you, and give you a look which said: "Fancy having HIM — and for a whole week."'

On his return from Sunderland, Benny had found cheap lodgings in a boarding house in west London, and as he sat in a deckchair in the garden he had plenty of time to think about just what he wanted to do.

The aspiring comics with whom he had mixed on his discharge from the Army — Max Bygraves, Bob Monkhouse, Tommy Cooper, Norman Wisdom — were all doing well with regular radio spots and increasingly good slots on music-hall variety bills.

Benny himself hadn't done too badly on radio. He had appeared on *Henry Hall's Guest Night* with Reg Varney, and also done solo spots on shows like *Variety Bandbox*, *Beginners Please* and *Midday Music Hall*.

The problem with radio was that it didn't pay very well. The only real money to be made was in live summer shows or touring variety, and the Sunderland saga had so embittered Benny that he wasn't sure he would ever want to face a live audience again.

Benny had always been a prolific comedy writer, producing ideas for his own act, sketches for revues and a whole series of visual gags which had worked well when he was partnering Reg Varney.

Now, pondering his future as he sat in the suburban back garden, he wondered whether some of them might work on TV.

'I began writing some sketches with television in mind,' he remembers. 'They were sketches about people I had seen, real-life incidents with people on buses, in the street or in restaurants.'

In three weeks he wrote about 40 sketches. Then, the thick bundle of comedy material tucked under his arm, he caught a bus to BBC Television's Lime Grove studios and asked to see Ronnie Waldman, the head of light entertainment.

It is highly unlikely under the present-day set up at the BBC that so highly placed a person as the head of light entertainment would agree to see an unknown comic wandering in off the street.

But things were much more informal in 1951. For one thing, television was already displaying its voracious appetite for new material and Waldman was intrigued to hear that the young gentleman called Benny Hill who was at the front door requesting an interview had brought some TV scripts with him.

Seated behind his polished oak desk, the BBC boss looked with some amusement at the eager-faced, fair-haired young man who placed a pile of handwritten scripts in front of him.

'I'd like you to read some of these,' said Benny. Then, thumbing through the stack of scripts as though they were a pack of cards, he requested: 'Tell me when to stop.'

On a nod from Waldman, Benny pulled a page from the pile and went to hand it to the BBC man for him to read.

'No,' said Waldman, waving it away. 'I don't want to read it. You work the sketch for me, let's see what it looks like.'

'Me?' gulped Benny, looking somewhat anxiously around the empty office. 'Here?'

Waldman nodded and sat back expectantly. Benny took a deep breath, muttered 'Well, here goes' and sailed into the sketch. It was about a man putting his tray on a conveyor belt in a Lyons tea shop, and the BBC executive found himself chuckling as Benny frantically mimed his way through it, scurrying to keep up with the imaginary conveyor belt, desperately trying to catch falling crockery while still holding on to his bowler hat and umbrella and apologising as he bumped into irate customers. Ronnie Waldman thumbed thoughtfully through the batch of scripts as Benny sat opposite him, panting from his exertions in the make-believe tea shop.

'Who do you think these sketches might suit?' asked Waldman.

'I don't know, I thought you might have some ideas,' replied Benny.

'You know,' suggested Ronnie. 'I think they might suit you. Would you like to perform them on TV, Mr er ... what did you say your name was?'

In fact, though he didn't say so at the time, he knew very well who Benny Hill was. He had seen him fleetingly two years earlier, when Benny made his first ever TV appearance on a show called *Music-Hall* with Alfred Marks and Vera Lynn.

'I wanted to kick the furniture,' observed Waldman. 'I knew Benny had something that was just right for TV, but he was doing the wrong sort of act — just telling a stream of jokes.'

Why Waldman didn't follow up that original hunch and invite Benny for a TV audition remains a mystery. But he made up for lost time by getting Benny together with his deputy at the BBC, Bill Lyon-Shaw, and Benny was featured in a TV show called *Hi, There*. Produced by Bill Lyon-Shaw in August, the 45-minute programme cost just £400 to make.

'They couldn't very well call it the Benny Hill Show, because nobody had really heard of Benny Hill,' admits Benny.

Unknown though Benny may have been, his appearance on *Hi, There*, in a series of solo spots and sketches impressed at least one national TV critic.

The *News Chronicle* reported: 'Mark down Benny Hill among the future TV favourites. He's aged 26, is fair-haired, and has more than a mere idea of what makes visual fun.

'If neither his material nor his background was brilliant, Benny demonstrated that given the help of an experienced script writer he could be one of the brightest comics on TV.'

Such complimentary reviews, however, did not exactly add up to overnight success. But they were encouraging enough to endorse Benny's feelings that TV was where his future lay, and he continued to write material which was more suitable for the small screen than the stage.

But he didn't neglect radio entirely. A show called *Anything Goes*, which was produced in the BBC's West Region studios, caught the attention of the *Sunday Chronicle* radio critic who observed: 'I swear Mr Hill and his show have between them something which, in the long run, may cause Messrs Ted Ray, Dickie Murdoch, Kenneth Horne and Frankie Howerd some anxiety.'

And there was a hint of things to come when the *News Chronicle*, reviewing the same programme, said: 'One word of warning. The script at times has a tendency towards *double entendre*.'

In 1952, Benny did an audition at the Nuffield Centre, a venue he remembered from his wartime days. Tucked away off Trafalgar Square, it was a service club where men and women in uniform on leave in London were entertained by variety shows at which many of the performers were young entertainers using the date as a showcase for the various agents and bookers who found the Nuffield a useful source of new talent.

The informal atmosphere of these shows, with the overspill audience sitting on the floor, had prompted the BBC to use it as the background for a live televised programme called the *Centre Show*.

When Benny did his audition at the Nuffield Centre, BBC producer Kenneth Carter was in the audience and it struck him that the chirpy young comedian with the expressive face would make an ideal compère for the TV show.

That proved to be a very shrewd judgement. Benny's breezy style struck just the right note with the young Nuffield Centre crowd, and the likeable young comic who played to the camera made an equally pleasant impression on the growing television audience who tuned in to the programme — by the beginning of 1953 more than two million sets had been sold.

Most successful entertainers can look back on a particular piece of luck or unexpected happening which turned out to be a crucial element in their success. For Benny Hill such a totally unpredictable turning-point came during his tenure in the *Centre Show*.

One night he walked on stage at the Nuffield Centre and beckoned confidentially towards the TV cameras. 'I have a police message here,' he said, reading from a piece of paper. 'A football pools coupon was lost last night in Chelsea. Will anyone who finds it, please contact Scotland Yard, telephone Whitehall Home-Away, Home-Away.'

It was a perfectly innocent gag. The famous phone number of Scotland Yard was Whitehall 1212. On a football pools coupon, the figure one meant a home win and the figure two was an away win.

If the laughing Nuffield Centre audience found it good harmless fun, someone highly placed in Whitehall certainly didn't. Amazingly, an anonymous complainant from official circles had read something sinister and sexual into Benny's football pools gag.

He insisted that Benny had actually said Homo-Way, Homo-Way, thus insinuating that homosexuality was rife in Whitehall.

What was even more surprising was the fact that department AG3, the Services entertainment unit, took the protest seriously.

A complaint signed by a War Office colonel was sent to the Nuffield Centre Management Committee, on which all three services were represented.

'I'm flabbergasted,' said Benny. 'All I know is what

the BBC have told me — that some brass hat objected to the joke. They must have misheard me because they said that home-away had something to do with sex. I'm quite sure there was nothing suggestive or improper.'

Plastered all over page one of the *Daily Mirror*, this storm in a Whitehall teacup set the entire nation laughing. But it didn't stop the Nuffield Centre committee taking an equally grave view of the situation. They wrote to the BBC insisting that in future they should be allowed to vet every *Centre Show* script before it was screened.

Understandably outraged by this ludicrous reaction, Ronnie Waldman refused. Indeed, the BBC light entertainment chief was so disgusted and angered by the whole affair that he decided to quit the Nuffield Centre altogether and put an end to the *Centre Show*.

The BBC had recently acquired the old Shepherd's Bush Empire to use as studios, and Waldman decided that the replacement for the *Centre Show* would be transmitted from there.

The new programme would be called *The Services Show*. And its regular compère would be Benny Hill.

Building on the popularity of the *Centre Show*, and cashing in on the publicity which the row over the football pools gag had engendered, Benny eagerly seized the opportunity the BBC had given him.

'Thank goodness the BBC haven't sacked Benny Hill, even if that War Office colonel doesn't approve,' said the *Daily Mirror* after the first of the new shows was screened from Shepherd's Bush.

By now perfectly at home in front of the TV cameras, Benny came across as one of television' s most relaxed and polished performers.

'He's the sort of nice-looking young chap you can help liking,' suggested Ronnie Waldman.

But producer Kenneth Carter knew better than anyone that behind Benny's amiable, almost casual approach lay a very shrewd understanding of the special techniques needed for TV.

'He has the gift of being able to underplay, so important in television,' enthused Carter. He can be funny with a glance, or the raising of an eyebrow.

'I honestly think he's the best compère in Britain. He has a tremendously warm personality which registers even better on TV than in the theatre.'

That personality was obviously having a widespread impact. *The Sunday Pictorial* TV critic, reviewing one of Benny's appearances on *The Services Show*, wrote: 'Of all the up and coming comics I name Benny Hill as the surest for the big time. He looks good. He invents very funny characters. He has enough of them to ring the changes on his act. And he THINKS television.'

It was this last factor which was the key to Benny's success. He was one of the first comedians to realise, as Ronnie Waldman had done some years earlier, that the traditional stand-up patter which comedians employed on the music-halls was just not suitable for television.

There was something dreary and lifeless about a man at a microphone delivering a string of gags, many of which were well past pensionable age.

Television called for a new approach, more inventiveness and, above all, something entirely fresh for every appearance.

With his ability to write most of his own material, Benny was one of the few comics who could produce tailor-made segments for TV.

'The future of entertainment lies with TV,' Benny told TV columnist Fred Cooke. 'That's the star to which I've hitched my wagon.'

His huge success on *The Services Show* led to him being featured as the star of a new Kenneth Carter comedy programme called *Show Case* in 1953.

Benny was under orders from Ronnie Waldman to develop character comedy, with the promise that if he was successful there would be the possibility of his being given his own show.

He spent hours in front of the mirror, rehearsing expressions and pretending that he was looking into the TV camera. It was a diligence which paid off handsomely.

Show Case proved to be the perfect vehicle for Benny's versatility, an opportunity at last to display the full range of his considerable talents.

His gift for impersonation and mimicry, first revealed so many years before when he began imitating the music-hall performers he saw at variety theatres when he was still a schoolboy, now became the focal point of a show whose approach was entirely different from anything that had gone before.

The main targets for this wickedly observed mimicry were television personalities who had become household names as TV increased in popularity and began challenging radio for the broadcasting audience.

A flamboyant hairdresser who called himself Mr Teasy Weasy had become the darling of the housewives through his numerous TV appearances in which his exaggerated gestures and colourful clothes had provided a welcome change from the somewhat stiff presentation of most television performers.

On *Show Case*, Mr Teasy Weasy became Mr Twirly Whirly as Benny flounced in front of the cameras in an outrageous wig, satin-lapelled smoking jacket and flowing bow tie.

Grabbing models by the scruff of the neck, hacking a new hairstyle out of a household mop and periodically blowing kisses to the camera, Mr Twirly Whirly was a sensation.

'I call this hairstyle the Ebb Tide cut,' he simpered, putting the finishing touches to a creation which looked like a badly made bird's nest. 'It has all the warmth and gaiety of a piece of dead seaweed.'

Benny appeared also as television chef Philip Harben, in beard and butcher's apron. 'Now,' said the chef, 'take this cup of herbs. I'm sure Herb won't mind us using his cup.'

The public loved it, and so did the television critics. Leslie Ayre in the London *Evening News* commented: 'His art is not so much that of the impersonator as the caricaturist, unerringly picking out this and that foible and playing it up with a fine sense of the ridiculous.'

And another critic added: 'He is one of the very few personalities on TV who could play the condemned man, the firing squad and the officer giving the order to shoot with the lift of only one eyebrow.'

Praise poured in from all directions. 'He is positively the most original and refreshing comedian that British TV has discovered,' purred Moore Raymond in the *Sunday Dispatch*.

An episode of Show Case in July 1954 had Clifford Davis eulogising in the *Daily Mirror*: 'Mr Hill gets better and better. He was so entertaining that all the other acts in the programme almost faded into nothingness.'

And *Reynolds News* raved: 'Here was an avalanche of laughs, mass produced by a young man who behaves on our screens with an enthusiasm which can only indicate that rare creature — a person who really believes that there's a future for him on TV.'

Suddenly, Benny Hill was in the big time. Fan mail, scripts and offers for summer seasons and variety tours poured in. He was earning £300 a week, massive money at a time when the average national wage was less than £10 a week and businessmen earning £1,000 a year were considered quite comfortably off.

Yet the money made no difference to Benny's modest life style. 'I've never known anyone of his age to be such a steady spender,' marvelled his agent, Richard Stone.

The nation's No. 1 comic still travelled by tube, and two attractive teenage girl fans who were delighted when Benny invited them to lunch were somewhat surprised when the meal turned out to be an inexpensive snack at a little café off Trafalgar Square. Then he bought the girls a quarter pound box of chocolates and took them to a news cinema.

This was followed by tea and cakes in a snack bar,

whereupon Benny announced that he had to dash because he had a performance to do. 'It's 25 minutes by tube to the theatre,' he explained, looking at his watch.

Couldn't he take a taxi?

'Oh, I could,' said Benny. 'But it would cost me 10 bob.' Benny confessed that, in spite of his huge earnings, he was still only spending at the rate of a £10 a week man. 'Who knows?' he said. 'In a few years' time I might BE a £10 a week man.'

He was living in a £3 a week room at a bed and breakfast boarding house in Kilburn, west London. 'He's the cheeriest guest we've ever had,' reported his landlady, Mrs Connie Rhodes. 'But he spends hours alone, watching television and writing. A lot of the time my Pekingese dog, Peeko, sits with him.'

Inevitably, there came a time when Benny needed more space. His bed-sit was cluttered with contracts, scripts, sheet music and letters from admirers.

'It's ridiculous, there's hardly any room for a television set,' he complained.

So Benny moved — to a slightly bigger room in the same house.

Delighted by the runaway success of *Show Case*, Ronnie Waldman kept his promise. In September, 1954, the BBC announced that Benny would star in his own show in the New Year.

'The Battle of Benny Hill (1953–54) has been won,' exulted the TV writer for the *News Chronicle*. 'It seems that by sheer dogged persistence in their loyalty to the 28-year-old comedian of *Show Case* the customers have forced TV to give him his own series.

'Why Mr Hill has not received the call before remains a mystery. Mr Ronnie Waldman, head of light entertainment, cries out that comics willing to tackle a series are rare birds; that good writers capable of feeding them with scripts are almost as scarce.

'Under his very nose for 18 months has been Mr Hill, introducing the acts in the *Centre Show* and later *Show Case* and more often than not making those pottering programmes worthwhile by sheer weight of his own personality and the original fizz of his wit.

'Furthermore, Mr Hill writes all his own scripts. In at least a show a month since January 1953 he has not had a flop. This week in *Show Case* he towered over his mediocre supporters with a burlesque on *Quite Contrary* which was the biggest laugh since Arthur Askey.

'Television, scraping for comedy talent, persisted in the ridiculous statement: "We are grooming him for stardom." They have been grooming, with a rather worn brush, a man whom the public have long considered a star.

'The extraordinary thing is that it should have taken the man who has probably provided more good TV fun than any other single artist two years to be offered a show of his own.'

There was only one snag about Benny's new programme. What should they call it?

Supposedly snappy names like 'Spotlight' and 'Curtain Up' were proposed and rejected.

'We need something simple, something that will tell the viewers exactly what to expect,' suggested Ronnie Waldman.

'Let's call it *The Benny Hill Show*.'

Outside the Sunderland Empire the queues stretched right round the block.

Benny Hill was top of the bill, and the crowds waiting in the cold chattered excitedly at the prospect of seeing in person the television comic whose weekly shows were becoming compulsive viewing for the entire country.

Coat collar turned up and hat pulled down over his eyes, Benny Hill watched them, unrecognised, from the other side of the street. It was hard to resist a smug little smile.

Sunderland Empire was where his show business career had almost ended in disaster, the variety theatre where the audience had booed him off the stage in the days when he was touring with Reg Varney. Now he was back, his name emblazoned in letters four foot high across the front of the elegant old music-hall.

Benny's spectacular success on television had led to a series of offers for him to tour in variety, but he had consistently turned down such suggestions. However, towards the end of 1954 the money being offered for these dates had soared to more than £500 a week.

Benny agreed to take a stage show out on the road — on the condition that one of the theatres they would NOT play was the Sunderland Empire which still conjured up bitter memories of his night of humiliation.

But his agent, Richard Stone, pleaded with him to change his mind, shrewdly realising that the nightmare of that Sunderland experience would continue to haunt him unless he returned to lay the ghost of failure.

'Go back to Sunderland,' urged Stone. 'It will be different now, you'll see.'

And different indeed it was.

Strolling on stage to thunderous applause from the packed theatre, Benny deliberately included in his act the same seven-minute segment which had fallen on such stony ground a few years earlier. Only this time there was no slow handclap. The audience rocked with laughter, shouting for more.

The local newspaper confessed itself somewhat puzzled by this rapturous reception, commenting drily: 'Although we thought Benny Hill had a certain charm and was very amusing, we did not think his material warranted cheers and claps every time he stopped to breathe.'

If Benny Hill needed any confirmation of his enormous popularity, the three-month variety tour provided it. Theatres sold out weeks in advance and at some of the bigger venues Benny's contract, which was based on a percentage of the profits, netted him £1,000 a week.

Popular though he was, he was now confronted by yet another big challenge — his own television show. With actor Jeremy Hawk as his straight man, Benny began rehearsals at a students' hostel in Bloomsbury in London. Running through sketches beneath the green-shaded lamps of a draughty dance hall, he kept out the cold by wearing beneath his blue blazer a yellow pullover knitted for him by his mother in Southampton.

The first *Benny Hill Show*, with material mainly written by Benny himself, was transmitted from Shepherd's Bush in January 1955. Opening with some merry-go-round music first heard at a fairground in Chichester, the guest stars were singer Alma Cogan and comedienne Beryl Reid.

Eight million viewers tuned in, anticipating something special, but to Benny's dismay, the programme was far from being a runaway success.

'The show was patchy and lacked cohesion,' sniffed Clifford Davis, television critic of the *Daily Mirror*. 'A sketch in which Mr Hill appeared as a German farmer fell flat.'

The *News of The World* was similarly unimpressed, commenting: 'It was a night of great expectations, the night of Benny Hill's biggest break. Millions of families made the show a "must date". Most of the critics were disappointed and so, I believe, were many of Benny's most fervent fans.'

Other writers were equally uncharitable. '*The Benny Hill Show* was very nearly a flop,' warned Moore Raymond in the *Sunday Dispatch*. 'Benny wasted most of his talents on worthless stuff.'

Kenneth Bailey was equally blunt in *The People*: 'The show fell far short of our hopes. Benny was funny, but he had little new to offer.'

Such criticism left Benny uneasy and anxious. Television, which he thought could make him, now threatened to break him.

He sat for hours re-running the show, determined that if mistakes had been made they would not be repeated. And they weren't.

The following show, in February, was slicker, more polished and had much more pace.

'The show perked up with a bang,' admitted Clifford Davis. 'Here was Mr Hill in sparkling form.'

The programme included a hilarious take-off of the panellists on a quiz show called *Find The Link* and *The Observer* offered it this glowing tribute: 'If there is one word which describes the essential quality of good TV entertainment it is intimacy.

'It is here that TV has its supreme advantage over the theatre and the cinema. But there is only one light entertainment show that seems to have both grasped this principle and to be trying to act upon it — *The Benny Hill Show*.

'Benny would probably be a success in any medium, but he would never be so successful as he is on TV if he had not thrown overboard a lot of the technique which is successful on stage or screen but which, if one tries to get it into the living room of a suburban house on a Saturday night, is much too cumbersome and out of place.

Benny's mastery of the television technique had been watched with some admiration by Bob Monkhouse who, more than 30 years later, can still vividly recall the apparent natural ease with which Benny adapted to the new medium.

'Benny and the television camera fell in love with each other,' says Bob. 'The very inhibitions that made Benny a little uneasy in face-to-face human relationships worked to his advantage when he first saw a television camera.

'It was possible for Benny to be totally uninhibited with the camera, to wink at it, to make it his best friend and to be utterly intimate in what he was saying with his eyes and his slowly-spreading smile or mock astonishment or pretended innocence.

'All this came through the glass of the camera and into your living room and made him an intimate companion. No other comedians were achieving that at the time, with the notable exception of Arthur Askey who had the knack which he developed in concert parties of talking to small audiences, taking them into his confidence.

'Benny became the master of direct innuendo, straight into the camera. On television you could see the lowering of the eyelids, the little smirk, Benny's whole apparatus of physical tricks.

'Benny on radio seemed comparatively bland and less effective than he was on TV.'

By the mid-1950s, Benny Hill was emerging as the biggest and best-known comedian in Britain, and West End theatre managements scrambled to cash in on the incredible popularity of the fresh-faced young man from Southampton who could charm an audience with the wink of an eye.

Radio wanted him, too, and in 1954 he took over the part of the schoolteacher in the highly popular series, *Educating Archie*. The show was unique in that its 'star' was a wooden doll called Archie Andrews, manipulated by a ventriloquist called Peter Brough who could dispense with the problems of concealing his lip movements as the radio audience couldn't actually see him. Benny's predecessors in the teacher's role included Tony Hancock, Robert Moreton and his old pal, Max Bygraves.

In April, 1955, impresario Bernard Delfont signed

Benny for the Folies Bergère revue *Paris By Night* at London's Prince of Wales Theatre, starting with madcap magician Tommy Cooper. Although it was to run for more than a year, it didn't exactly take London by storm.

The *Manchester Guardian*, assessing Benny's performance in the lavishly staged production, concluded: 'His best work is done when parodying English and Irish folk songs, or as the speechless Yorkshire lad on holiday in Algiers whose appetite for romance in the casbah is blunted by demands for brass.'

For the first six months, Benny quite enjoyed the Folies show. He took great satisfaction in knowing that his dressing room was the same one once occupied by the great Sid Field. And, ever eager to learn, he was delighted to discover that his dresser, Bertie Lind, had been a singing comedian back in the 1920s, topping variety bills in Moscow, Tokyo, New York and the London Pavilion.

Although Benny was an established star, he wasn't too proud to pick up some hints from such an experienced old professional. 'Bertie has given me some priceless wrinkles about handling audiences,' he said.

But as the months went by the coach-loads of fans who flocked in from all over the country to see Benny at the Prince of Wales began to dwindle. The show had always been something of a problem for Benny because, for many customers, the beautiful girls in the show were the main attraction.

The home-grown audiences were replaced by foreign tourists who enjoyed the spectacular scenes featuring the statuesque girls but maintained a puzzled silence during Benny's performance simply because they couldn't speak English.

Benny's morale was revived when impresarios George and Alfred Black asked him to take over at short notice at the London Hippodrome where comedian Dave King, another early success on TV, had been playing to packed houses.

King had to have an emergency appendicitis operation, but the Saturday night audience knew nothing of this and were somewhat startled, if not disappointed, when Dave King failed to appear and Benny Hill stepped on stage instead.

Any misgivings they might have had soon disappeared. Benny, delighted to be back in front of a British audience who could actually understand his jokes, was in unstoppable form and put on a performance which earned him a standing ovation and the eternal gratitude of George and Alfred Black who had been as nervous as he was about how the paying customers would react to his last-minute substitution.

Successful though these stage outings were, Benny was reminded that his real strength lay in his TV performances when he was voted Personality of the Year for 1954–55 in the *Daily Mail* National Radio and Television Awards. Said *The Observer*: 'Of all the awards made in the *Daily Mail* competition the one which shows most sign that the nature of the TV medium is being understood is the award to Benny Hill.'

Crowning his success in that crowded and eventful year of 1955 was an appearance before the Queen and Prince Philip at the *Royal Variety Show* at the Victoria

Palace, alongside such stars as Lena Horne, Diana Dors, Johnny Ray, Tommy Trinder and the Crazy Gang.

Looking back on that momentous 12 months, Benny found it hard to believe that he had also somehow found the time to make a film.

Benny's television appearances had caught the eye of Sir Michael Balcon, the head of Ealing Studios, who thought the chubby-faced young comic would be ideal material for one of the famous Ealing comedies.

The story he had in mind for Benny was about a daydreaming ice-rink sweeper who spends all his spare time avidly reading trashy detective novels. The scenario opened with him breathlessly poring over a purple passage which began: 'Me, I like my dames soft. But this baby wouldn't have splintered if you'd hit her over the head with the Empire State Building. She unzipped her blood red lips and ...'

Comedy writer T. E. B. 'Tibby' Clarke, who wrote *Passport to Pimlico*, was recruited to provide the script and the director was Basil Deardon who had made many comedies with Will Hay and George Formby.

For Benny it involved a gruelling daily routine with a car calling for him at 6 am to take him to the studios for eight hours of filming, then rush him back to the West End for two shows nightly in the Folies revue. He confessed it felt like serving a three-month prison sentence, but was full of enthusiasm for the project.

'If this film is a flop, it won't be Ealing's fault,' insisted Benny. 'They couldn't have taken more trouble if I'd been Danny Kaye.

'I'm very thrilled, but rather nervous. It's a wonderful script into which Mr Clarke has put so much that is me. But I also have to do some straight acting, and that's a different kettle of fish.'

For their part, the film makers were delighted by Benny's aptitude for the big screen. 'He has a personality and comedy that are in direct descent from Bob Hope,' said Deardon.

Scriptwriter Clarke was equally enthusiastic, adding: 'Time after time he has taken one of my lines and given it 100 per cent more punch by his manner, his timing, the uncanny fun he can inject into visual movements.'

Clarke had gone to great lengths to capture Benny's characteristics, travelling with him on variety dates and sitting through his act time and time again to study his mannerisms and facial expressions.

The film, called *Who Done It?*, followed the progress of the dozy ice-rink worker who achieves his dream of becoming a private detective after winning £100 and a bloodhound in a competition run by a crime magazine.

Co-starring Belinda Lee and David Kossoff, it involved knockabout skating scenes, intrigue with microfilm and Soviet spies and a hilarious stock car racing sequence.

The movie was released in March '56 to fairly favourable reviews. 'Mr Hill bumbles through it like a huge and charming innocent born to be a victim,' said the *Daily Mail*. 'If he can find scripts as good as this one Mr Hill should have no difficulty in repeating on the screen his successes elsewhere.'

'A crazy comedy that will certainly collect the cash,' was the *Daily Mirror's* verdict and the *Daily Sketch* reported: 'The picture packs more gags into each of its 85 minutes than any offering since Mack Sennett's Keystone Kops.

But reviewer Harris Deans in the *Sunday Dispatch* wasn't bowled over. 'Benny Hill doesn't get much help from script writer T. E. B. Clarke,' he suggested. 'And he needed a lot. There are beginnings of laughs, as when he runs amok with a sandwich board, but they never become fast and furious.'

To coincide with the release of the film, Benny made a recording of a song called 'Who Done It?' which didn't exactly race up the charts. 'Neat and bouncy' was how the weekly newspaper *Reveille* diplomatically described it.

By this time Benny had reluctantly moved out of the boarding house in Kilburn and moved to a comfortable but modest top floor flat in an old-fashioned red brick apartment block in Maida Vale in north-west London, overlooking the Regent's Canal.

In one corner was a foot-high devil statue of Mephistopheles, bought in a flea market in Paris. 'He brings me luck with two things dear to my heart — money and girls,' Benny confided to visitors.

'He's become my girl guide. If a date asks where I got that horrible thing, she's OUT. But if she says, Coo, isn't he lovely, that's my girl.

'Since I began putting cheques behind him they've got bigger and come more often. Much more of this and I'll be giving him 10 per cent.'

He had also acquired a secretary, Mrs Jones, to deal with the mounting piles of mail which flooded in after every TV appearance.

Despite his newfound stardom, Benny remained amiably accessible to the gentlemen of the Press who could always rely on him for a lively line or two. Declining invitations to join show business writers for lunch, he would more often than not invite them instead to his apartment.

'I prefer eating at home,' he explained to Robert Tee of the *Sunday Express*. 'You go to a restaurant and get a quiet table in a corner, then somebody recognises you and starts saying things like: "Coo, look, he eats too."'

The success of his first television series had both public and producers clamouring for more. But once again Benny displayed a canny understanding of the dangers which surrounded performers who risked over-exposure on the small screen. In particular he had begun to realise the alarming rate at which TV devoured new material.

'I don't want to do second-rate shows,' he explained. 'I want to spend time writing and devising new sketches. I would sooner hear people say "I haven't seen him for a long time" rather than "Oh, not him again."'

In any case, it was time to slow down. 'When I first got going I couldn't get enough of it,' he said. 'I took everything that came along as if it was food and I was starving.

'I can remember Saturday nights when I did two houses of variety, with a TV show in between, then rushed off to do a late night cabaret or radio show.'

In fact it was another 18 months before he tackled a second series for the BBC, and then there was another long lay-off before he returned to the screen in 1958. It was a strategy which paid off handsomely.

Constantly concerned about the need for fresh material, Benny had teamed up with script writer Dave Freeman, a one-time sailor and ex-policeman who Benny had first met while working on the *Show Case* programme for the BBC.

Freeman, who at 6ft 3in towered over Benny, shared his new partner's somewhat relaxed and informal approach to programme planning. They dreamed up ideas while walking in Regent's Park. 'We talk over things we want to do in the next show,' revealed Benny. 'Then sometimes we sit and watch all the other layabouts who are watching us.'

Undisciplined though their methods may have seemed, the results were remarkable. After a *Benny Hill Show* in February, 1958, the BBC switchboards at the Lime Grove studios were jammed with congratulatory calls from viewers.

Benny had done an uproarious impression of anchorman Cliff Michelmore who hosted the popular *Tonight* news programme and he also delivered a series of devastating impersonations of pop people from the *Six Five Special* music show.

'I doubt if any TV star has ever reached such heights in comedy mimicry,' marvelled Kenneth Bailey in *The People*.

Nothing and no one was sacred from a thorough debunking by the irreverent Mr Hill. A much loved

BBC talent show called *Top Town*, in which teams of amateur entertainers competed against each other, was mercilessly taken apart with Benny parodying everything from a hapless tap dancer to an out of tune accordionist.

The ratings soared, and one programme in the series drew a record audience of 12 million, the biggest since the *Coronation Music Hall*.

More records were broken when Benny did a summer season on stage at Scarborough.

But Benny was never allowed to forget how vulnerable he was. He had set himself such high standards that any of his television shows which fell even the slightest bit short of expectations came under the critical microscope as though it were a national disaster in which Benny had somehow let the entire nation down.

Ironically, the public had got to know Benny Hill so well that his constant quest to break new ground and experiment with fresh ideas and different approaches sometimes disappointed those who felt more comfortable with some of his more familiar material.

After one of his 1958 programmes drew less than enthusiastic notices, Benny responded: 'As time goes on there is no doubt that it will become harder and harder to make TV audiences laugh. The medium eats up material at an alarming rate.

'All right, people say that in this show I wasn't the old Benny Hill. But supposing I had done some of my old acts? Then people would be asking why I don't find new ideas.

'The hunt for new material gets more and more difficult. But don't you think we're inclined to take it all a little bit too seriously?

'It seems to me that it's all getting slightly out of proportion. I'm a funny man, I hope, and all I say is that next time and at all times I'll do my best. If I fail, that's just too bad. But don't let's get all grim about it.'

In August, 1959, Benny was back in the West End of London, starring for Bernard Delfont and Emile Littler in a revue called *Fine Fettle* with singer Shani Wallis at the Palace Theatre.

Benny played 20 different characters in the show, including Lady Godiva's cheeky groom and a suburban space traveller, and he had to have a crew cut so his hair would fit under the numerous wigs he wore. In one sketch he played five different characters, producing a screamingly funny bit of 'business' in trying to hide a ball and chain that wouldn't come off his leg during one of the costume changes.

He was also the leader of the massed bands of the Milk Marketing Board.

'What composers do you play?'

'Well, Johann Sebastian Bach, to name only three.'

Theatre critic Dick Richards of the *Daily Mirror* didn't think much of the production, and sniped: 'It's very much a seaside show masquerading as a West End one.'

Be that as it may, Milton Shulman of the *Evening Standard* was in no doubt about Benny's contribution to the proceedings.

'His cherubic face, with its eyes fluttering like some berserk windscreen wiper, represents on the surface the orthodox little man buffeted and baffled by fate,' he wrote.

'But he brings to this traditional comic characterisation a secret, lip smacking irreverence which gives his humour a boisterous, even bawdy quality.'

There was no hotter property in show business than Benny Hill, but despite badgering from promoters who just couldn't understand why he didn't take advantage of his phenomenal popularity, Britain's biggest box office draw appeared anxious to do less work, not more.

He steadfastly refused to buy a car, explaining: 'If I did, my agent would only have me driving through the night to even more engagements.'

A summer stage show in Weymouth in 1960 was restricted to just two and a half weeks, and he refused several lucrative offers to star in pantomime.

'My agent says I am bone idle, and I am,' confessed Benny. 'I'm just a layabout. I don't break a leg to do more than I have to. If I wanted to, I could make £50,000 a year.

'Now, don't think I don't like money. I'm ambitious up to a point. But what's the good of being the highest paid comic in the business if all you get out of it is the worry of how far you could fall down?'

In fact, Benny wasn't really quite so idle as he claimed. It was in 1960 that he returned to film making. 'There is a special sort of prestige about films,' he theorised. 'If somebody sees a film actor like Richard Todd in the street they say: "Hello, Mr Todd."

'But because I talk straight to them in their own homes, when they see me in the street they say: "Hiya, Benny." Mind you, I'm not complaining. It is quite something to play to millions of people at a time.

The film this time was *Light Up The Sky* and his co-star was cockney rock 'n' roll singer Tommy Steele, a former merchant seaman from London's Bermondsey district who had become so popular that he was hailed as Britain' s answer to Elvis Presley. With a supporting cast which included Ian Carmichael, Harry Locke and Dick Emery, the story was about life on an Army searchlight battery during World War Two. Benny and Tommy Steele played a music-hall double act who had been called up for active service.

It was not the most memorable of movies. Halliwell's Film Guide looks back on it now as 'a very patchy entertainment'.

As if finally acknowledging that he had 'arrived' as an entertainer, Benny moved out of his Maida Vale flat and took a lease on an apartment in Queen's Gate in Kensington, near the Albert Hall.

It was his only tangible concession to stardom and the fact that he was probably the best paid comic in the country. He still walked to work, rewarding himself with the occasional Mars bar if he thought he had shed any weight in the process.

The nameplate on the doorbell of his apartment read 'A. H. Hill', providing a permanent reminder that Benny Hill, superstar, had once been Alfred Hawthorn Hill, milkman.

And he remained entirely approachable to his newspaper friends from Fleet Street, welcoming them into the sparsely furnished apartment to chat over a glass of wine.

'A milkman's idea of heaven is a morning in bed,' he

told one visitor. 'So when I moved into this place I told the furniture people: "When you get round to the bedroom, just make it all bed."'

Benny had taken up playing the harp. 'I have a new one on order from South America,' he informed one show business writer. 'It's costing me over a hundred quid, plus postage. You must come to one of my musical evenings at the flat.

'We turn off the telly, and we all play harps. Or there's my record collection. I go for that rather weird stuff that comes out of South America. You know, pops from the past from Peru and Paraguay.'

But the opportunities for such musical evenings were few and far between. The television boom had been boosted when the BBC's monopoly of the medium ended in 1955 with the advent of commercial television, which carried advertisements or 'commercials'. By 1969, some 60 per cent of British adults were tuning in to TV every evening.

Benny was so much in demand that the 1960s turned into one of the most hectic periods of his life as Britain's top television personality continued not only with his television shows but also branched out into TV commercials, records and major films.

Every so often, however, he insisted on applying the brakes to this show business helter-skelter. He agreed to visit Australia for some personal appearances after his TV shows became popular 'down under', but took eight weeks to get there, stopping off at several exotic destinations en route.

He was away from Britain for more than four months in 1962, mainly meandering around the

Continent. 'I wasn't worried about the financial side of things,' he confided to a reporter on his return. 'I maintain my earnings at around £20,000 a year. I do around 12 television shows a year, never tour, and do a little radio.

'While I'm abroad, my records and television commercials keep the pot boiling and stop people forgetting me. I'm not a big spender. My flat costs about £10 a week, I don't run a car, don't drink much and smoke only about three cigarettes a day. So there's plenty of cash left over to invest.'

The records which Benny mentioned had done much to boost his already widespread popularity. Benny had occasionally featured comedy songs in his television shows, and in January, 1961, the Pye record company persuaded him to put one of them on disc. It was called 'Pepys' Diary', but it was the song on the 'flipside' which really caught on. 'Gather In The Mushrooms' had a slightly saucy lyric about a young man going courting in the country, and its sales benefited greatly when it was revealed that the BBC had seriously considered banning it because of its cheeky words.

'I don't know in this day and age what's rude and what isn't,' mused Benny. 'It's hard to know what entertainment is any more. Look at television — the other night they had Adolf Eichmann on one programme, and gallstones on another.'

The Mushroom Growers Association, delighted with the publicity for their product, presented Benny with a hundredweight basket of mushrooms.

'Hmmmm,' said Benny. 'I must think about doing

a song about Rolls-Royces next.'

The success of the mushroom song was quite quickly followed by another hit record called 'Transistor Radio', a rock 'n' roll number about a young man whose amorous approaches were constantly being interrupted at the crucial moment by his girl-friend's pocket radio.

Benny had written it when he had an hour to spare after missing a bus to Marseilles while on holiday in France. It gave Benny the opportunity to do several impressions, including a mawkish take-off of Elvis Presley's 'Are You Lonesome Tonight?' soliloquy and a waspish impression of orchestra leader Victor Sylvester hosting an overseas record request programme in which he played favourite tunes for listeners in such far-flung corners of the Empire as British West Hartlepool. On the reverse side was a number called 'Gypsy Rock', delivered at express speed.

'No, I'm never tempted to sing love songs,' Benny told an interviewer. 'I can only get by with a funny.'

Exercising his usual caution about over-exposure, Benny then carefully rationed his recording dates, spacing them out some 12 months apart. 'Harvest Of Love, again with a country courting theme, got into the charts and when Bob Dylan became popular Benny couldn't resist doing a send-up called 'What a World' which was all about a folk singer who sings protest ballads about poverty and injustices and then drives home to his penthouse in a Rolls-Royce.

'No, I'm not angry and I haven't got anything to protest about,' declared Benny. 'I just thought it was time for a funny folk record because they get terribly serious about it, you know.'

The record was included on an album entitled 'Benny Hill Sings?', the cover of which showed Benny in a black polo neck sweater peering down his nose with a John Lennon look.

But perhaps his greatest success came with a song for which he drew on his experiences some 25 years earlier in Southampton.

'Ernie: The Fastest Milkman in the West' reached number one in the *New Musical Express* best seller charts in 1971, beating artistes like Slade, Cher, Olivia Newton-John, Tom Jones and Diana Ross.

It was all about the adventures of a milkman on his daily round, and there was even a mention of Market Street, the road down which Benny had driven his horse when he was delivering milk as a teenager.

The song was such a smash hit that Benny was invited to perform it on the *Top Of The Pops* television show. He politely declined. 'Imagine me standing there singing surrounded by all those trendies,' he said. 'I would have looked a right idiot. It would have been trespassing. I would have been out of place. It's for the kids, and I am anything but a kid.'

Still, he did agree to make a short film for *Top Of The Pops*, guiding a horse and cart round the streets of Maidenhead while the record played in the background.

While there was no denying Benny's brilliant versatility, even he was surprised by the offer he received in 1964. At a cost of £20,000, an unprecedented sum in those days, ITV planned a television production of Shakespeare's *A Midsummer Night's Dream*. A distinguished cast including Jill Bennett, Anna Massey, Patrick Allen, Alfie Bass and Bernard Bresslaw had already been signed.

Now they wanted Benny Hill, to play Bottom.

'You must have got me muddled up with someone else,' spluttered Benny, when the producers telephoned. But there was no mistake. Director Joan Kemp-Welch thought he'd be ideal for the part.

'I've seen the play performed a couple of times, and I must admit the thought of playing Bottom had crossed my mind,' conceded Benny. 'But only in the way you might think about marrying Brigitte Bardot — too fantastic.'

At least he knew this was one production where he could rely on the script writer. 'Shakespeare was pretty witty,' he pointed out. 'Can you imagine the gags of today lasting 400 years?'

Benny was understandably nervous about performing in such distinguished company. But he needn't have worried.

'Benny Hill made his Shakespearean bow as Bottom,' said the *Daily Mirror* review. 'And the performance he gave was TOPS.'

The critic added: 'He acted with rustic conviction. He made a perfect ass in the scene with Titania and the fairies, a role that calls for no little ability.'

This acting ability was also put to good use in a series of cameo roles in major movies throughout the 1960s. In 1968 he was to be found at Rothenburg ab der Tauber in Germany, decked out in knickerbockers, grey wig and leather braces for his part in the £4 million film *Chitty Chitty Bang Bang*, starring Dick

Van Dyke. Benny played the part of an old German toymaker leading a gang of urchins against a dastardly robber baron who was trying to get his hands on a magic car which could float and fly.

The following year he played a lecherous Italian computer expert, Professor Simon Peach, bribed to snarl up the Turin traffic while a gang led by Michael Caine staged a daring bullion robbery in *The Italian Job*.

Earlier he played Fire Chief Perkins in *Those Magnificent Men In Their Flying Machines*, a knockabout comedy centred round a London to Paris air race with a cast which included Red Skelton, Sarah Miles and Tony Hancock.

While such acting jobs were undoubtedly good for his prestige, they didn't do as much for his bank balance as the series of TV commercials Benny undertook for the Schweppes soft drink company.

Disarmingly frank about the income which these advertisements brought him, he said: 'For five years I made more cash from the commercials than from anything else.

'I got a fantastic amount of money. The contract involved me in two weeks' work a year, for which I received enough to live in luxury for the rest of the year without doing a stroke. Ridiculous. People in this business are hopelessly and idiotically overpaid.'

Some clue to just how much money Benny was making emerged in December, 1967 when a Stock Exchange company bought Benny Hill Productions and Benny received shares worth £140,000, a small fortune at that time. The company was expected to make a profit of at least £250,000 in the following five years.

Uncharacteristically, Benny celebrated by buying the flat next door to his in Queen's Gate and having the two knocked together into one big apartment at a cost of £20,000.

The television commercials, while producing a handsome income, also performed a useful professional purpose. Returning from a tour of Australia, Benny observed: 'After a trip down under you expect to come back and find people saying: "I thought you were dead, mate." But the telly ads kept my face on the screen.

Nevertheless, Benny continued to carefully ration his appearances on the small screen, often taking months off to prepare new material for his shows. On one occasion he vanished for several weeks, and then surfaced to disclose that he had been wandering around the Camargue region of southern France 'going for coach tours and getting nicely sloshed on red wine'.

He added: 'I've also been doing some writing. I supply all my own material, and I'd run out. In television you've got to be startling nowadays, otherwise people forget you've been on. It's not enough merely to put on a good routine show.

'I'm always looking for something that people will remember for at least 24 hours. I've got to keep them talking about Benny.'

Television tastes were changing, and Benny wondered whether he should get away from the format in which he relied heavily on his hilarious impressions.

They were still popular enough, but performers like Tony Hancock, Eric Sykes and Harry Worth had established themselves in situation comedies which were commanding very big TV audiences.

Collaborating with script writer Dave Freeman, Benny decided in 1962 to embark on a series of shows in which each episode would centre on a different theme. One of them was *Portrait of a Bridegroom*, in which Benny played several versions of the same bridegroom, as seen through the eyes of various people at a wedding.

Another, called *The Before Man*, featured him as a sad advertising film director in a series of guises including an airline pilot, a Mountie and a racing driver.

Then there was *The Constant Viewer* in which he portrayed Bert Noggsmith, a bricklayer's mate who is a TV addict and gets personally involved with the plots, picturing himself as Dr Kildare or a genius violinist or a super-intelligent quiz programme contestant.

He also appeared as a reporter, sent to interview a crusty old colonel (also played by Benny) at his country home.

Once again Benny ran into the perils of daring to do something new. Well written though they were, these character roles were not universally well received.

After Benny appeared as a broken-down body builder called Mr Apollo, the *Daily Sketch* TV critic gibed: 'All the best artists grow up and mature. But on this showing the immature Hill of five years ago was nearly five times as funny.

When the BBC signed him to a £12,000 contract

for eight 45-minute shows in 1965, he took an entirely new tack. 'I'll be getting away from the situation comedy I have been playing,' he announced. 'The shows will be a mixture of odd comedy sketches, funny quickies and musical interludes.'

It was a winning formula. With Benny's genius for taking even the oldest gag and giving it a fresh twist in a song or a sketch, the shows fairly romped along and they led to Benny being named BBC Television Personality of the Year in 1966.

His programmes also developed an interesting new 'edge'. The occasional sharply observed impersonation of a major TV personality was still included, but these ran side by side with sketches which almost seemed to amount to laughter-coated barbs aimed at the foibles of a pretentious, materialistic and selfish society.

This development did not escape the discerning eye of the *Daily Mirror's* television critic who observed: 'In a restaurant scene he was in turn and simultaneously, and at once, the man who took the beauty to dinner, the waiter who served her and the female violinist who serenaded the eaters. Not to mention the commissionaire at the door.

'What were his targets? Money. Pomp. Self importance. Greed. In short order he sent up the lot.'

Benny's success with the BBC had always been enviously eyed by the commercial television companies. He had made various appearances on ITV over the years, but stayed loyal to the BBC and resisted tempting offers from the independent companies to sign long-term contracts with them.

In 1969, however, he made the move which would eventually take him to international stardom. He signed a deal to appear exclusively for London-based Thames Television, and immediately began work on four colour spectaculars, in one of which he delivered a riotous send-up of the Eurovision Song Contest with Benny appearing as different contestants from six different countries.

He also did a Christmas Day special, grappling with professional wrestler Tommy Mann, despite the fact that just before the sequence was filmed he sprained his ankle badly tripping over a camera cable.

But it was his first comedy series for Thames, in 1970, that contained the main ingredients of a magic mixture which was to turn him into one of the best-known comedians in the world.

Benny, in turn, was the blundering buffoon, the cheeky chappie with a slightly saucy song, the Chaplin-like figure in a speeded-up sequence fashioned on silent films and the leering lad who never quite gets the girl.

Such a simple but effective formula charmed television critics like Leonard Buckley of *The Times*. Reviewing a *Benny Hill Show* in March, 1970, he wrote: 'Most television comics outstay their welcome. But not so Benny Hill. Not for him the guest appearances, the constant grinning from some plug for margarine.

'He rations his performances. So he comes to us fresh. And fresh he is. The fatuous face exudes good health. He is every mother's notion of a well-nourished son, a walking, talking advertisement for apple dumplings and early to bed.

'But the fatuousness is important too. He is the ham-fisted dolt we have all encountered — the plumber who flooded the basement, the mechanic who scratched the car.

'In short, he is television's Oliver Hardy. And we love him for it.'

In March, 1970, the hour-long *Benny Hill Show* on Thames Television was watched in 9.25 million homes, which Thames said was the highest national viewing figure for any programme shown on ITV over the previous two years.

It was claimed that the only programme to have a higher rating during those two years was a BBC production of Miss World. *The Benny Hill Show* had even pulled in more viewers than the Apollo moon landing.

While writers struggled to analyse the show's phenomenal success, critic Stanley Reynolds neatly captured Benny's personal appeal when he observed: 'If there is a joy in watching Benny Hill, I think it comes from the madman's pleasure he has in his own efforts. He appears to be only just this side of the asylum gate.'

CHAPTER
FIVE

Behind the Scenes

Packed full of American tourists, the big bus edged slowly down the narrow road alongside the River Thames in Teddington, just outside London.

Eager with anticipation, faces peered excitedly out of the coach windows as they cruised cautiously down Broom Road until, suddenly, the magic moment was upon them.

'And here it is, ladies and gentlemen,' said the tour group courier, talking triumphantly into a microphone with the air of a man about to arrive at some hitherto unattainable journey's end.

He pointed proudly past a uniformed security guard on duty at the nondescript entrance to what looked like a large industrial estate.

'Thames Television studios, home of the *Benny Hill Show*.'

In an instant the bus was ablaze with the flash of several dozen cameras going off together. As the bus slowed, the American visitors scrambled to get off for a closer view of the studios and the chance to take even more photographs to show the envious folks back home.

'Along with Buckingham Palace and the Tower of London, our Teddington studios appear to be well and truly on the American tourist route,' laughs Dennis Kirkland, producer and director of the *Benny Hill Show*. 'Hampton Court is only just up the road. So they do that in the morning, then head here.

'They know all about the *Benny Hill Show* from seeing it on television in the States. And they all want to see the very spot where the programmes are made. It's almost like a pilgrimage.'

Had this particular bus-load of trans-Atlantic pilgrims not been so busy capturing the somewhat featureless scene on colour film they might have noticed a small, sandy-haired man carrying a plastic bag full of shopping slip quietly through a side gate.

With a friendly nod to the commissionaire, the new arrival disappeared quickly through the main door, smiling slightly to himself at the antics of the Americans who were now bombarding the security man at the front gate with questions about just which building was the actual home of the *Benny Hill Show* and pleading to be allowed just the briefest of peeks inside.

The man with the plastic bag made his way to a modest dressing room in Studio One, dumped his shopping on the table and hung up his jacket behind the door.

From his pockets he took a bundle of handwritten notes, scribbled on scraps of paper.

Benny Hill was ready for work.

'Benny's not the kind to sweep up to the studio in a huge limousine like some showbiz superstar,' explained Dennis Kirkland, a former floor manager who has been producing the show for seven years and is one of Benny's few close friends.

'Of course we offer to lay on a car to bring him out to Teddington. But more often than not he prefers to make his own way out here, often walking the last few miles and doing a bit of shopping en route.'

Benny's contemporaries in the entertainment world can never get used to the idea of Britain's highest paid TV performer walking to work. 'There was a time when Max Bygraves was driving to the studios in his Rolls-Royce when he saw Benny trudging down Teddington High Street with a bag full of groceries,' recalls Kirkland, an amiable character in sweater and jeans.

'Max stopped his car and yelled: "What's the matter, Benny, too skint to afford a cab?"'

While Benny's deliberately low key arrival to start making a new series may seem somewhat incongruous for a millionaire entertainer whose programmes are shown all over the world, it is typical of the workaday beginnings from which a *Benny Hill Show* is produced.

For this is no Hollywood-style production in which batteries of scriptwriters and assorted ideas men sit earnestly closeted for months on end dreaming up new material for The Star.

Producer Kirkland well remembers that the origins of one *Benny Hill Show* lay in the arrival on his desk of a dog-eared piece of cardboard covered with what looked like Egyptian hieroglyphics.

'It was one of those cardboard stiffeners you get inside a new shirt,' Dennis recalled. 'And it was smothered with almost incomprehensible scribbles in Benny's handwriting, which is not very good at the best of times. At first we thought it was some kind of secret code, but then we deciphered a note from Benny scrawled down the side.

'It explained that he had been sitting outside a cafe in Madrid when he suddenly got this idea for a sketch about a Chinese waiter. What Chinese waiters have got to do with Spain we never did discover.

'Anyway, when Benny got back to his hotel he wrote it all down on this piece of cardboard and stuck it in the post. The dialogue was all this jokey flied lice, lookeee-lookeee-me-no-likeee Chinese chat, which is why we had such a job unscrambling it.

'In the end we managed to make some sense of it. And it turned into a brilliant sketch.'

Benny's impulsive habit of writing down an idea as soon as it strikes him has resulted in numerous notions arriving at the Teddington studios jotted down on anything from a Malaysian restaurant menu to a Bangkok beer mat.

'He'll scribble something down on a cigarette packet and send THAT to me if he can't find anything else to write on,' says Dennis, 'and he always carries a newspaper with him, so he can scribble in the margins.'

Such ideas are buzzing through Benny's brain months before a new show goes into production. Some of his best material is dreamed up while he is

sitting outside a Continental cafe on holiday, surveying the passing scene. The antics of a strolling guitar-
ist in Spain or a harassed gendarme in Paris could well
provide the inspiration for a sketch which will eventually end up on the TV screen.

Over the years such observations have given birth to
the never-ending procession of madcap characters
who march through the *Benny Hill Shows*. Mr Chow
Mein, the 'sirry irriot' Chinaman gives way to Mervyn
Cruddy, the perennial talk show bore. Professor Otto
Stumpf, the old Bavarian buffer inspired by Benny's
wartime service in Germany, is followed by Pierre de
Terre, the avant-garde French film director.

A white-coated Scottish doctor with a meandering
mind lectures earnestly on the vagaries of the human
race: 'I once knew a native girl. All she wore was 11
beads, and eight of them were perspiration. She didn't
tell me she had a glass eye — it came out in conversation. Her feet were so big, she had to go to the cross-
roads to turn round.'

The bowler-hatted loon extolling the benefits of 'a
nice genital way of life' is replaced by a straw-chewing
village idiot intoning: 'They've got a new vicar up at St
Paul's. He don't half talk a lot of nonsense.'

In between, the brave boys of the Lower Tidmarsh
Fire Brigade rescue scantily clad maidens from burning buildings and a choir of singing railway porters
steam their way through Widdicombe Fair ('old
Uncle Tom Cobblers and all').

And at every turn is the ubiquitous Fred Scuttle,
constantly at our service with his peaked cap crazily
askew, eager eyes blinking madly through wire-

rimmed glasses and fingers enthusiastically splayed in a ragged salute.

Fred Scuttle, too, was born out of Benny's military service — he had to wear similar little round glasses as a driver during the war. Scuttle made his first appearance, as a test pilot in a wheelbarrow factory, on one of Benny's BBC shows in 1956.

Garnished with Benny's wit and inventiveness, the most insignificant incident can turn into an eminently workable idea for television. On one occasion, Benny was listening to a band in Kensington Gardens in London when he noticed a young woman relaxing with her eyes closed, dreamily conducting the band with one finger.

It gave rise to a sketch where everyone in the park was playing some imaginary instrument, led by a conductor with his eyes closed using a newspaper as a baton.

'I'm so busy scribbling things down that in restaurants I'm often mistaken for one of those undercover spies from *The Good Food Guide*,' admits Benny. 'But when an idea hits you, you MUST write it down, otherwise it can go out of your head. I'm never without a pen, and I'll reach for the nearest scrap of paper when I need to make a note.

'When people who want to be scriptwriters say to me "I've got a few ideas I'd like to discuss," I always say: "write them down."

'I might spend 26 hours on a plane travelling to Australia. But that doesn't worry me. I take my exercise books, and on each line I write something. If it takes more than one line, it's probably not worth doing.'

It is from this rag-bag of vague ideas, partly written sketches and one-word suggestions for a few seconds of visual 'business' that the internationally acclaimed *Benny Hill Show* begins to take shape.

Some of the jokes date back to his boyhood, remembered from the days when his father used to take him to the music-hall in Southampton and honeymoon sketches were very much in vogue.

'Just Married' says the large label on bridegroom Benny's suitcase in one of his TV skits. 'And Don't You Forget It' reads a similar label on the luggage of his hatchet-faced 'bride'.

'He has an amazing memory for gags,' says producer Kirkland. 'And he never wastes anything. He will save a gag for years, waiting for the right slot to put it in.'

This ability to re-cycle material in different ways so as to wring every last chuckle out of it is not lost on his professional colleagues.

Comedian Bob Monkhouse, who has no mean memory for jokes himself, recalls writing for the radio show *Calling All Forces* back in 1951 when Benny, then an up-and-coming comic, appeared with film star Diana Dors and funnyman Arthur Askey.

'Benny did patter gags in that show,' says Bob. 'Some 10 years later I saw him on TV delivering the same series of jokes in exactly the same order, only this time they were in a song. He had taken the gags and woven them into a lyric.

'I have noticed he does this again and again, reworking the same basic ideas. I have sat there dumbstruck with admiration at the switches he has pulled.

'And why shouldn't he? Good gags are like jewels.'

Max Bygraves, another entertainer who has watched Benny develop over more than 40 years, is similarly impressed. 'He's a very fine comedian,' says Max. 'What amuses me is how he can keep permutating the same dozen gags.'

Benny himself is the first to admit that many of his jokes are re-worked gems from the past. Once asked to reveal his favourite joke, he trotted out the well-worn tale of the Member of Parliament who was visiting a mental home and was amazed to discover that a beautifully designed flower bed was the work of an inmate.

'I can't believe there is anything mentally wrong with someone like you who can do such wonderful work,' the MP told the patient. 'I shall arrange for your immediate discharge and get you a job as a gardener somewhere outside.'

As the MP hurried off to the hospital offices, he was suddenly knocked almost unconscious by a brick thrown by the inmate. 'Don't forget, will you?' asked the grinning gardener.

While fellow professionals may be understandingly tolerant of a comic who can give old material a new shine, those less personally concerned with the difficulties of creating new scripts are not always so charitable.

Television critic Chris Dunkley groaned with displeasure when Benny insisted on reviving one particular old chestnut in one of his early shows for Thames Television.

Writing in *The Times*, Dunkley commented: 'When I was about four my mother managed to reduce me to an almost hysterical fit of giggling by promising to show me her new water otter and then producing a kettle.

'Benny Hill trotted out the same joke in the first of his new series on Thames, and somehow its age and weakness, almost its senility, seemed to serve as a touchstone for the entire show.'

Yet, only a short while later, it was this very ability to dust off well-used items and put them back in the comedy shop window which intrigued another Times writer, Leonard Buckley.

'Benny Hill's routines remain the same,' Buckley acknowledged. 'There is nothing extraordinary about them. He sings. He recites. He takes part in a sketch. Where he scores is the inventiveness with which he invests the same old thing.

'When he comes home in the sketch to discover the other man he is at once a master of outrage: "He's got my individual fruit pie!" When he comes to his recitation he is the countryman using the humans to explain to his son about the birds and the bees.

'Of course Benny Hill can be saucy. But it is all disarmingly done. "I don't believe in that sort of thing before marriage and I'm not sure about it afterwards either," he told us primly in one scene.

'After that reassurance he could have pinched Mrs Grundy's bottom and still have had her, like the rest of us, shaking with mirth.'

Ideas, both old and new, are what come under discussion when Benny and producer Kirkland meet some three months before a new programme goes into rehearsal. They get together over a meal, a favourite venue being the Royal Garden Hotel in Kensington where Benny spills out suggestions in between courses of spicy, oriental food which Benny has acquired a taste for during his travels in the Far East.

But such informal planning sessions are just as likely to be conducted at the humble Indian tandoori restaurant near Mr Kirkland's home just outside London.

Scribbling on the back of serviettes, the two men begin to rough out the format for a new show, adding a joke here, a sight gag there. By the time they reach the coffee and brandy stage, an outline has begun to emerge.

A rough script is produced, but seldom rigidly stuck to. Says Kirkland: 'We are always adding things, gags that suddenly strike us to make a scene even funnier, an additional sequence that will bring an already promising script to life.'

Production begins in earnest at one of several hired rehearsal rooms. One is at Richmond rugby ground. Another is at Hampton Court, in the banqueting room of the Charlton Hotel. It's a deliberately chosen unobtrusive location, and few outsiders know that it is used by Benny and his team.

Here, with red and blue tapes crisscrossing the polished dance floor to mark the positions of cameras and performers, the cast comes together for the very early run through of sketches, songs and production numbers.

As they tentatively tackle the raw material to the accompaniment of just a piano, Dennis Kirkland busies himself with the endless details necessary to bring the show together.

But as events progress in the green-walled rehearsal room it is quite obvious that there is really only one 'guvnor'.

And that's Benny Hill.

He's the first to admit his key role both behind and in front of the cameras. 'I write the script, choose the music and write the original songs,' says Benny. 'I sing my own songs into a tape recorder with a guitar. Sometimes on the cassette I'll include a record of somebody else singing an entirely different song, just to give some idea of the orchestration I have in mind.

'Then I get together with our musical director, Ronnie Aldrich, over a drink, and we work out the music between us.'

To the outsider it is hard to imagine that such fragmented beginnings will eventually produce a television show which will be seen in almost every corner of the globe.

'There's never any fuss or the kind of circus atmosphere which you might expect to find surrounding a very big star,' says Jacqueline Bellone, whose father owns the Charlton Hotel. 'You'd hardly even know that Benny Hill is here.'

But Benny Hill is there all right, calling everyone 'dear heart' and meticulously rehearsing every line over and over again until those scribbled notes on the back of old envelopes gradually begin to turn into sketches and scenes which will have audiences chuckling from Sydney to San Francisco.

His never-ending search for new bits of 'business'

extends to occasionally turning up with impromptu props which he carries in yet another plastic bag (this passion for plastic bags led to the cast giving him an expensive leather briefcase for his birthday. When he opened it, he found it was full of plastic bags).

Benny was delighted when he discovered that plastic egg boxes realistically produced the sound of a bone-crushing handshake, and insisted that this sound effect should be incorporated in a sketch.

'I'm not trying to do the effects people out of work,' he points out. 'It's just that I want to be a part of everything that goes on.

'And as the one who dreams up the ideas, I know just how I want things to be done.'

During rehearsal breaks, Benny and the cast sometimes pop next door to the Cardinal Wolsey, a homely, working class pub featuring a pool table and the kind of red and gold flock wallpaper much favoured by Chinese restaurants.

Several pictures of personalities from the show line the walls, including a large framed photograph of Benny dressed as a sailor, arm in arm with veteran character actor Bob Todd who is togged out in a wedding dress with the skirt hitched high above his knobbly knees. 'To Toddy, my favourite bride. Luv, Benny Hill,' says the handwritten inscription scrawled across the bottom of the black and white photo.

Back in the rehearsal room they run through a sequence featuring pocket-sized Irishman Jackie Wright as a little old man trying to dig a tunnel from Britain to France. The script calls for the project to dissolve in chaos, with a cement mixer churning out black puddings, several people getting blown up when the doddery old tunneller accidentally sits on a high explosive detonator and the little old man finally digging his way up through the floor of a beach hut where a gorgeous girl is wearing bikini briefs and clutching a tiny towel to her bosom.

Enter Benny, as an apologetic beach attendant who offers the young lady his profuse apologies for this outrageous invasion of her privacy.

'May I shake your hand?' he inquires, by way of atonement. As the girl reaches out with her hand, the towel falls off. It's simple, its saucy — and it's fun.

The bones of the sketch are worked out there in the rehearsal room. The special effects will be filmed later, on outside location and in the studio.

Some sketches will require quite elaborate sets, such as the inside of a Wild West saloon or the dining room of a swish restaurant. Others get by with a simple prop or two, reminiscent of Benny's music-hall days. A French setting, for instance, might be suggested by a simple signpost saying 'Paris, 2 Miles' or a street sign labelled 'Rue de Postcard'. 'We just give a new twist to funny situations,' insists Benny. 'We don't use too much dialogue. It's not necessary. It's the actions which speak for themselves. If something is funny, really funny, then it appeals to everyone — no matter where they live, and whatever language they speak.

'We do a lot of non-dialogue stuff in the shows. I can remember one programme where we opened up singing on board a ship, and that was followed by a sketch with no words at all. A man in Afghanistan could have understood at least half of that show with no trouble at all.'

But if it's dialogue that's needed, Benny Hill has a never-ending supply of one-liners, hand-written on foolscap sheets.

'Why do you keep scratching yourself?'

'Because I'm the only one who knows where it itches.'

'How did you come to hurt your leg?'

'I didn't come to hurt my leg, I came to mend the roof.'

'I gave my secretary the sack. She said: "I'll do anything if you'll forgive me." So I forgave her — four times.

Though that mythical man in Afghanistan might be baffled by such quickfire corniness, he would have no difficulty following the sketch in which Benny is seen lustily patting the backside of a crinoline-clad lady.

All eyes are on this seemingly outrageous behaviour until a large dog, which had really been the object of Benny's bottom-patting affection, emerges from behind the crinoline.

Criticisms that such sequences are vulgar and basic evoke no argument from Benny. 'That's the humour I like,' he concedes. 'It's very traditional, like a seaside postcard.'

In the somewhat severe surroundings of the Hampton Court rehearsal rooms, such seaside postcards are brought to life. Raspberries are rasped, belches are belched, and flatulence is implied as an earnest clergyman who is supposed to be delivering the epilogue on television squirms in a leather chair which emits the most embarrassing noises.

But it is also the birthplace of some cleverly con-structed sketches like Benny's memorable parody of the hit movie *The Sting*. Benny's version was called *The Catch* and featured Benny as the boss of an inept gang of country bumpkins made up of Bob Todd, Henry McGee and Jackie Wright.

'You don't think, do you Arnold?' rages Benny at one of these henchmen. 'When we did that bank job and I told you to put something on your face, I didn't mean Brut aftershave for men.

'And what about your grandfather? Confessed to a life of crime on his death-bed and then got better.'

Puffing on a large cigar, little Jackie Wright ob-serves: 'I see they're looking for a cashier down at the bank.'

'But they took on a new one only last week,' protests Benny.

'Yeah, that's the one they're looking for,' says Jackie. 'He was six foot tall and £10,000 short.'

Henry McGee, meanwhile, is transfixed by the spectacular cleavage of Benny's gangster 'moll'. 'Funny,' he murmurs. 'I always thought good things came in threes.'

Also on hand at the rehearsals are the famous Hill's Angels, the eight-girl dance group whose cleavage, bottoms and stockinged thighs are the subject of so much close-up camera work.

In the finished show they will appear in a series of skimpy costumes, dressed as anything from French maids to mini-skirted traffic wardens. During these early rehearsals, though, they work through their rou-tines in an assortment of tights, leotards and leg warmers, looking more like a football team in training than Britain's sauciest dance troupe.

The original Angels were formed in 1979, after the success of a raunchy take-off of the Hot Gossip group in one of Benny's TV shows set him thinking that similar segments could spice up the programme on a regular basis.

Hundreds of ambitious young girls fancy themselves as Hill's Angels, but from the avalanche of applications, few are chosen.

'Benny is very hard to please, the perfect professional,' says Sue Upton, the 30-year-old blonde who is the longest serving Angel and who now supervises recruitment of new girls for the leggy lineup.

'If a girl has a flair for singing and dancing, that's a start. But she has got to find the comedy funny herself to take part in Benny's sketches.

'He likes them petite. He doesn't mind if they're blondes or brunettes so long as they have that certain indescribable twinkle that comes across at the audition and on camera.

'He doesn't especially want big boobs, only if they are suitable to accentuate a certain sketch — like when he leers at them as Fred Scuttle.'

Sue made an early impact on Benny when she was dressed up as a granny, dodging wheelchairs in a crazy chase sequence which he had devised for TV.

'It was when the Belisha beacon fell on her head at a zebra crossing that I realised I had a girl with talent,' recalls Benny. 'Sue is really funny. But finding pretty girls who are talented and funny is not easy. Not all girl dancers are pretty. Some of them I have to sit and talk to for an hour, encouraging them and advising them on their future. I mean, you just can't say: "Sorry, dear, you look like me in drag."

'And a lot of girls don't fancy all sorts of things being poured over them and generally having to wear very little during filming, especially in the bitter cold.'

Although the Hill's Angels frequently appear in skimpy costumes, Sue Upton insists that they are never expected to wear or do anything which they find embarrassing. 'If they think a costume is too revealing, they've only got to say so,' she says.

One girl who did feel embarrassed was the appropriately named Sharon Fussey, who refused to wear a very revealing string bikini for a beach sketch. 'It was just ridiculous, it barely covered you,' protested 18-year-old Sharon. 'I told Benny straight that I wasn't going to do it.

'He was very sweet about it, and said: "O.K., dear heart." Then they got another girl to do the scene.'

This surprisingly amicable settlement of a potentially contentious situation came as no surprise to Sue Upton. 'In all the years I've known Benny I've never heard him swear, raise his voice, lose his temper or say anything disrespectful to a girl,' she claims.

It is Benny himself who has the final say on every costume worn by the girls. 'He can't bear a girl to be blatantly erotic,' points out Louise Walker, a designer responsible for many of the Angels' most stunning outfits. 'She has to look sexy, but with a vulnerability and an air of innocence about her.

'It's the same with the costumes. We can get away with see-through dresses and suspenders, but Benny draws the line at going topless.

'It's the girls who make the outfits really work. Put an ordinary girl into some of our gear and she'd look like a sack of potatoes.'

Benny insists that the girls were not originally chosen to be outrageously sexy. 'I didn't want the men saying "Cor, look at that" and the wife saying "I wonder what's on the other side",' he explained.

However, there were quite a few comments of 'Cor, look at that' when the Hill's Angels, wearing very revealing costumes cut high up the thigh, did a dance routine set in a gymnasium in January, 1981. There were protests both from the public and some of the girls themselves.

'Hill's Angels Revolt' screamed a headline in the *Star*. 'Halo, Halo — Benny Hill's Angels in Sex Storm,' blazed the *Sun*.

The protests centred on a group of women office workers from Sheffield in Yorkshire who complained that in this particular sequence the Angels were lewd, rude and downright disgusting.

'We are not prudes, we are not even women's libbers,' said 28-year-old Pauline Johnstone. 'We are just girls who think that Benny's dancers are going too far.

'Things are so bad that some of our husbands are embarrassed. We feel sorry for the dancers. They were wearing next to nothing, and the cameras kept shooting in for close-ups of their bottoms.'

Another of the Sheffield protesters, 26-year-old Maureen Ryan, added: 'Most of us find Benny amusing, but his Angels are just being used as sex objects. We think there is a limit to how far the show should degrade women.'

Claire Smalley, one of seven Hill's Angels who took part in the gym scene, was equally outraged. 'We did wear very daring costumes,' she admitted. 'But when I saw the finished thing, I was horrified. Most of the dance routine had been cut. I had no idea the cameraman had been zooming in so close to certain parts of the body. The scene was far too provocative and suggestive. My friends were shocked at what they saw.'

Claire added: 'I suppose the show does go a bit too far at times, but it's all innuendo. We all know what Benny's humour is like, it's all very tongue in cheek.

'I have never refused to take part in any of the routines, but if I am asked to do this sort of thing again I will refuse even if it means quitting the series. I feel we have been exploited. I don't want to be shown in that way.'

Despite the controversy gleefully whipped up by the tabloid Press, producer Dennis Kirkland was unrepentant. 'Benny and I resent all the fuss,' he said. 'We can't deny the girls are sexy, but what's wrong with that?

'We certainly don't go out of our way to be dirty, and the girls certainly weren't naked. If people have dirty minds, that's their problem.

'I received only three letters of complaint out of 20,000,000 viewers. As a result of all this fuss in a couple of newspapers I expect the IBA [Independent Broadcasting Authority] will be watching us like hawks. But they won't find anything dirty.'

While rehearsals for a new show continue at Hampton Court, a production team at the Thames studios in Teddington busies itself seeking out suitable locations for outdoor filming, preparing special effects and designing sets and scenery.

The designers and wardrobe department are confronted with one of the world's weirdest shopping lists, paraphernalia and special effects required to make Benny Hill's imaginative sketches come to life. Required items include exploding underwear, collapsing cucumbers, stuffed bulls, man-size bird costumes, disintegrating teapots, lifelike dummies to be tossed from the top of tall buildings, nuns' habits, motor cars which appear to have no driver, bicycles which fall apart at the slightest touch, a Mona Lisa portrait which squirts water, Batman costumes, advertising posters which come to life, whoopee cushions, cotton wool mouth pads for a Godfather impression and a television set which walks across the floor like a robot.

Playing a sketch as Wonder Girl, Sue Upton was wired up so that she could confront the 'Baddies' by throwing open her cape to reveal a built-in machine-gun in her bra.

'When the gun went off it was like a minor explosion,' she said. 'I thought I was about to lose part of my vital equipment. I fully expected my nipples to be scorched.'

For a skit on Carmen, set in a cigar factory, designer Jan Chaney ordered a supply of genuine tobacco leaves only to discover that they began to crumble when exposed to the air. She solved the problem by coating them with a rubber solution so they could be handled by Benny and Co. without falling apart.

Her search for a dog with two heads ended with the

discovery of a mild-mannered terrier who didn't mind having a false head fixed to his backside.

The make-up department is also on full alert, ready to transform the demanding Mr Hill into anything from a grey-haired Chelsea pensioner to a swashbuckling pirate with a wooden leg.

'Benny is meticulous about make-up and wardrobe,' says Dennis Kirkland. 'Even if it's for a segment lasting just a few seconds, he will insist that he creates an entirely new character with the right make-up, wig and clothes to fit the situation.'

Such attention to detail dates back to his days with the BBC. Doing a send-up of the long running *Coronation Street* soap opera, he sensed one essential ingredient was missing from his impersonation of the fearsome Ena Sharples, caretaker of the Glad Tidings Mission Hall. So he asked Granada Television if he could borrow Ena's threadbare old coat which actress Violet Carson wore in the show. Granada obliged, and Benny went in front of the cameras confident that at last his impersonation of Ena was complete.

Make-up girl Pearl Rashbass recalls the programme where Benny decided to appear as the hulking Mr T in a spoof of the *A-Team* television show. 'I took four hours to do Benny's make-up,' she says. 'The headpiece was composed of about 10 different rubber and latex pieces.

'But Benny was really patient. Still, that's what he's like. He doesn't care how long something takes as long as it is 100 per cent correct in the end.'

Despite the gruelling routine of early rehearsals in the wood-panelled banqueting room of the Charlton

Hotel, there is an atmosphere of fun and light-hearted mateyness about the proceedings.

'They are like a big family who have grown fond of each other over the years,' explains Mick Rhind, a former Thames Television publicity officer who worked on the *Benny Hill Show*.

'Benny and his producer, Dennis Kirkland, are so much on the same wavelength that they both seem to know instinctively whether something is right or wrong without actually having to talk to each other about it.

'And he is surrounded by experienced professionals like Bob Todd and Henry McGee who know just what Benny wants to get out of any given situation.'

Henry McGee, a very experienced stage actor, has been playing straight man to Benny for almost 20 years. 'He is an absolute delight to work with,' says Henry. 'He's intelligent, knows exactly what he wants and never loses his temper.

'You know, actors are sometimes better educated than comedians, but comedians are often wiser men. Shakespeare spoke of a man being wise enough to play the fool, and that describes Benny precisely.

'He has a brain like a laser, and a mind completely without cobwebs. He always goes straight to the core of the problem, without any unnecessary fiddling around the edges.'

Bob Todd, another veteran of the show, is a former Royal Air Force gunner and wireless operator who flew more than 130 missions over Germany in Wellington and Lancaster bombers during World War Two.

He survived five crash landings, demonstrating a resilience which has been constantly required on the *Benny Hill Show* where he has been repeatedly soaked with water, battered with anything from a lady's handbag to a policeman's truncheon, covered in slime, spaghetti and soup, buried up to his neck in sand, flung through the air in bar-room brawls, dangled from the branches of a tree and thrown from the back of a bucking bronco.

'Benny generates a tremendous amount of fun while the programmes are being made,' says Bob. 'It is impossible to look at his face closely for more than a few seconds without laughing.

'Then, suddenly, EVERYONE will be laughing helplessly, and the shooting on that particular sketch will have to be postponed until the afternoon when everyone has calmed down.

'But beneath it all one senses the extremely meticulous and careful way he has put the scripts together. They are always easy scripts to work from, because he writes only for you, knowing exactly what you can and can't do.

'I have acted in comedy most of my life. I think Benny Hill is a comic genius. He is like Spike Milligan — his mind works in a different way from most people. He has to find some way to make it intelligible, and he finds an outlet in comedy.'

Keeping a straight face on camera while Benny is within smirking distance is a constant hazard for the performers. 'I remember in one sketch I had to sing 'La Vie en Rose' while Benny had a daydream about me,' said former Hill's Angel Louise English. 'The only way I could stop myself from laughing was to dig my nails into the palms of my hands, and by the end of the scene I had the marks to prove it!'

Dressed simply in sports shirt and slacks, Benny Hill seems to be everywhere in rehearsals, especially when the action moves to the studio floor at Teddington. Peering through the camera lens, suggesting a change of pace in a sketch which seems too slow, explaining how the addition of a hat or a pair of glasses will wring an extra laugh out of a comedy sequence, he is totally involved in almost every aspect of the production.

Sketches which don't quite work are hastily re-written on the spot. Jokes are added, extended, polished, projected. And more than 35 years after he first began to demonstrate his mastery of television comedy, Benny is still picking up technical tricks of the trade which will add to the impact of the finished show.

'It's extraordinary what a tiny change of speed will do for a sketch,' he reveals. 'I replay some of my shows to see if I could get an extra laugh or two by literally altering the pace. Sometimes just deleting a few frames will add perkiness to a routine.

'Another time you might want to achieve an Alfred Hitchcock effect, so you slow it down by a couple of frames and the whole thing becomes thoroughly eerie.

'I get a tremendous kick from watching people like Charlie Chaplin and Jacques Tati. Slowing down some of the classic scenes from *City Lights* and *The Gold Rush* shows how much attention to detail went into Chaplin's seemingly straightforward slapstick routines.'

Preparations for the *Benny Hill Show* move into a more unpredictable and less manageable phase when outside filming begins at locations which have encompassed everything from a monastery to a medieval castle.

Dennis Kirkland ruefully recalls the occasion in 1979 when they rented a Tudor mansion near Windsor to film a spoof of *The Three Musketeers*. The owner stipulated that he must be paid extra for every day the filming ran over schedule and Thames Television, anticipating no major delays, agreed.

What they hadn't bargained for was a strike by TV technicians which halted all commercial television production. The Benny Hill sets, complete with lighting equipment and scaffolding, had to be abandoned in the grounds of the mansion until the dispute ended more than two months later, by which time the owner of the house had clocked up a nice little bonus of almost £2,000.

'There are other things we have had to leave around because of the strike,' said a plaintive Kirkland. 'We seem to have lost a western town somewhere, and if anybody finds one in a field, it's ours.'

Much of the outdoor filming is done at the plush Lensbury country club, next door to the Thames studios at Teddington. Members and staff there have become used to seeing Benny tramping through the grounds dressed as a Scoutmaster in oversized shorts or creeping through the undergrowth togged out as Tarzan.

On occasion, filming at the club is interrupted by the gentle curiosity of patients from a nearby mental hospital who wander over to see what all the fuss is about.

Among them is a gentleman of military bearing whom the production team immediately nicknamed The Colonel. Their first encounter with him came when The Colonel marched smartly into the middle of a sketch featuring Benny as an Indian Army officer on the NorthWest Frontier.

'That man!' bellowed The Colonel, pointing an accusing finger at Benny in his oversized pith helmet, ludicrously baggy trousers and puttees. 'Improperly dressed! Sergeant Major, take his name! Atten-SHUN. Quick march — left, right, left, right, left ...'

The bemused Benny soon decided it was best to humour the intruder and went along with these parade ground orders until it was tactfully suggested to The Colonel that it was really time he retired to the officers' mess.

The old soldier retreated with a smart salute and a final, disapproving glance at Benny's unkempt uniform.

Most outside sequences at the Lensbury club are shot without dialogue, a necessary restriction because of the jumbo jets which constantly drone overhead on their way in to land at London's Heathrow Airport.

Such silence was golden when, to film the sequence of Benny as Mr T in the *A-Team*, location manager Sandra Brown hired Elvetham Hall in Hartley Wintney, Hampshire, the one-time home of Henry VIII's wife, Jane Seymour.

Benny roared round the extensive grounds on a moped, several pounds of 'gold' chains swathed round his neck. Bob Todd, playing a villain being chased by Mr T, was required to plunge into the muddy waters of a four-foot-deep lake.

Splash! A hefty push from Mr T sent the reluctant Mr Todd flying into the murky waters.

The craggy faced actor, half drowned, staggered spluttering up the bank only to receive another hefty shove which sent him slithering back into the lake.

Floundering around in the weed-covered water, he looked up, seeking direction.

'Ad lib!' yelled Dennis Kirkland, and Mr Todd responded with an appropriately fruity string of blush-making adjectives which would definitely not be included in the finished version of the sodden scene.

'Sometimes we will film all day and get only a minute or two of footage which will eventually be used,' says Kirkland.

'Benny will often do as many as seven different characters in a day. It's very demanding and time consuming. But Benny wants to get it right, and he'll take the time to make sure he does so.'

Benny himself is always on the lookout for suitable locations which might inspire a sketch, or situations which can be developed into an amusing sequence.

He spends hours tramping alone through the New Forest near his Southampton home, dreaming up ideas. Sometimes he'll take similar solitary strolls on the Isle of Wight, where he went on holiday with his family as a youngster. He loves agricultural shows, and at one of them he saw a display by the Flying Gunners, the Royal Artillery motorcycle team.

With the Army's permission, he recruited the motorcyclists for a sketch set amid a South American revolution, with the Flying Gunners zooming in and out at high speed and Benny in the thick of things. Having learned to handle a motorcycle in the Army, he insisted on doing his own riding, although a soldier doubled for him in the more dangerous stunts.

By and large, the Benny Hill which viewers see on screen is the genuine article, but occasionally he uses a stand-in for risky bits of business like a fireman sliding down a pole head first, a cowboy being thrown off his horse or a parachutist crashing through a roof.

'Benny is too valuable a performer to chance being injured,' says Ken Seddington, an athletic actor who has stood in for many of Benny's stunts and who can be seen briefly in his own right in the familiar speeded-up climax to the *Benny Hill Show* in which a collection of scantily clad ladies, dwarfs in long shorts and other assorted odd-balls chase Our Hero in jerky double-quick time.

While great care is taken over potentially dangerous sequences, there is no accounting for hidden hazards. Benny once had a narrow escape while playing a milkman whose float was supposed to suddenly disappear while his back was turned.

A crane had been hired to lift the float out of sight, after which Benny was to wander around looking baffled and searching for it.

The float was still suspended in mid-air when, in between takes, Benny walked forward to talk to the director. Crash! The hook holding the float overhead snapped, sending the delivery cart hurtling down on the spot where Benny had been standing only seconds before.

'Looks like the drinks were almost on me,' quipped Benny, shaken but unhurt.

But there is little time to dwell on such incidents. The deadline for the new show approaches, and already the segments filmed on location and in the studio are being edited for transmission. A quickie item showing Rembrandt painting a nude model by following the numbers marked all over her body has worked well, and will be included.

So has a restaurant scene in which Benny appears as a doddery old musician in a band of strolling players, craftily sticking glue on the end of his slide trombone so he can reach out and pick up pound notes from the tables when the customers are distracted while paying their bills.

The two-headed dog is fed at both ends, Bob Todd appears as a nun with a moustache and Benny smirks and flutters his way through a spoof on a Swedish sex film ('Hotte Sex, Free Loff and Lust Orgie').

It is decided that a song which Benny sings as a Spanish father sending a letter to his son in jail in Valencia should be saved and performed live in front of the studio audience.

The lyrics, penned by Benny in a pavement cafe in Barcelona, are vintage Hill:

'Your mother's gone back on the coal round.
She's coming home tired as hell,
Oh stick it, I say, for just one more day,
Or until that old cart horse gets well.'

Meanwhile, in homes all over Britain some of the most sought-after tickets in show business are being delivered to people who have spent months and sometimes years on the waiting list for them.

The tickets carry a wide-eyed picture of the nation's most enduring comedian and the message which the fortunate few have been waiting for:

'Thames Television invites you to *The Benny Hill Show*.'

CHAPTER
SIX

Ladies' Man

Benny Hill surrounds himself with beautiful young women.

In his television shows he winks at them, leers at them, occasionally kisses them and frequently pursues them with apparent evil intent as they flee frantically from his lustful attentions, scantily clad and squealing.

The good-looking girls of Hill's Angels add spice and sex to a situation in which Benny Hill has become almost a fantasy figure living in a world which allows him unlimited access to long-legged ladies with big bosoms.

It is a scenario which has long fascinated show business writers seeking comparisons between the on-screen make-believe of the TV clown and the off-screen reality of bachelor Benny's private life.

The fact that Benny has never married has inevitably inspired innuendo and gossip in an industry where people's personal lives are an endless source of speculation and spite.

After a lifetime of fielding loaded questions from inquisitive interviewers Benny is not afraid to meet such speculation head-on.

'I know all about the rumours and what people say about me,' he told television journalist Clifford Davis. 'Some people think that because I'm not married there's something strange about me.

'But I'm not gay and I'm no weirdo.

'Of course I have occasional affairs with girls. Who doesn't? But I am always very discreet.

'I don't yell. I don't tell. And I'm grateful as hell.'

That last line, delivered with a cheeky, confidential wink, could have come straight from a Benny Hill script. Over the years he has produced a whole series of such jokey responses to fend off inquiries about why he is still single.

'Of course I'm looking for a wife,' he will insist. Then, with a sly grin: 'But I often think, why should I make one woman miserable when I can make so many happy?'

On other occasions his response has been: 'Why get married? I mean, you don't jump in a lake just because you are thirsty. Why buy a book when you can join a library?'

If all else fails, he resurrects the well-worn quip: 'I have a mental age of 17, and that's too young to marry.'

The fact is that Benny Hill has been unlucky in love. His first unhappy encounter took place when he was a 12-year-old schoolboy in Southampton and he was absolutely entranced by a pretty girl some two years older whom he first saw at a local fairground. He found out where she lived, and used to walk six miles from his own home just to catch an occasional glimpse of her.

But he was too shy even to speak to her, and it was almost four years later when he was working as a milk roundsman that he met her accidentally in a cinema queue and plucked up the courage to introduce himself. 'It came to nothing,' Benny remembers. 'Complete disillusionment. That's the story of my life.'

Such disillusionment was added to when, at the age of 25, he fell head over heels in love with a dancer in a summer show at Margate, Kent. 'I was starting out in show business and I had banked everything on becoming a success and marrying at the age of 30,' he explains. 'I had even thought about the kind of flat I wanted, and had it furnished in my mind from top to bottom.

'I just didn't think I was earning enough to keep a wife. I was making £20 a week and I had to pay £2 to my agent. And then there was the rent, and the cost of hiring second-hand dress suits for my act.'

Despite his misgivings about being able to support a wife, Benny was so smitten with the dancer who had caught his eye that he determined to propose to her. But he was too shy to do so face to face.

'She was in another show in the same town,' he says. 'I phoned her from a seafront phone booth in the interval and asked her to marry me.

'She said she was just going on stage, and would ring me back the next day at my digs after thinking it over. The next morning she turned me down. I was devastated.'

The aspiring young comic's dismay at being rejected was compounded when he learned the reason for the refusal — the girl was in love with somebody else, a Harley Street dental surgeon whom she later married.

'It was a terrible shock,' admits Benny. 'I was so big-headed I couldn't believe there COULD be anyone else.

'That affair really hit me. I locked myself in the lavatory and cried my eyes out. I even had a breakdown and had to go to bed and call the doctor. I was almost suicidal.

'For about three years I was a head-in-the-gas-oven case. When I look back, I find it difficult to believe that any woman could have had such a shattering effect on me. Benny boy has been awfully careful ever since.'

Benny has never revealed the name of the girl involved, just as he has maintained a discreet silence about two other ladies with whom he fell in love just as his career began to take off in the 1950s.

'They were both actresses,' is all he will say. 'I went from one to the other on the rebound, and then after things didn't work out they suddenly both turned up on TV at the same time on different channels. It was as if there was no escape.'

Despite this discretion, Benny couldn't stop the Press linking his name with every pretty girl in sight when his television appearances turned him into one of Britain's best-known entertainers in the '50s and '60s.

The sight of him dancing cheek to cheek with a 22-

year-old dancer called Norma Lewis in January '57 was enough for newspapers to start sounding wedding bells. Suggestions that romance was in the air became even more frequent when the couple were spotted cruising down the River Seine in Paris. 'Nark it, don't lumber me,' Benny protested to the *Daily Sketch*. 'You blokes are getting just like my Mum.'

Benny confessed that he and Norma were good friends, and hoped to be together in a summer show at Great Yarmouth. But he added cautiously: 'I'm not planning to marry yet.'

Some months earlier the girl in his life had been identified in the gossip columns as Doris Deal, a 25-year-old singer and dancer at the Windmill Theatre. They were reported to be seeing each other several times a week, and the delectable Doris was said to have taken him home to meet her parents.

'I have lots of girl friends and Doris has other boy friends,' said Benny, dismissing marriage rumours. And Doris chimed in: 'I'm very fond of Benny, but our careers keep us too busy to think of marriage.'

Playing guessing games with visiting reporters who clamoured for tit-bits about his love life became something of a speciality for young Mr Hill as the tabloid Press strove to satisfy public curiosity about the Southampton milkman who had set the entire nation laughing.

It was often difficult to separate fact from fiction as Benny mischievously fed them tantalising morsels which blossomed into equally titillating headlines like 'My ideal woman — by Britain's No. 1 Bachelor.'

'My ideal girl would have to be understanding, and

laugh at my jokes,' he told one interviewer. 'At the moment I send my gags to my Mum. If they make her smile, then I know I've got a winner.

'My biggest turn-on is a girl who can make me laugh, so that we can have fun together. I can't stand heavy vamps, and I suppose my ideal is someone like Goldie Hawn.'

The *News of The World* were predictably delighted when Benny provided them with details of a trip he had made to the Far East. 'It's very much a man's world out there, particularly in Tokyo,' he confided.

'Cor, do you know about those Geisha girls? They are brought up with one object in life, to make men happy. They kept saying: "Are you happy, Blenny?" By gorry, I was.

'It's far different back in London. The birds always take the same line. You know, what are you buying me for Christmas, or what expensive nightspot are we going to?'

At his London flat, Benny took great delight in rummaging through a drawer full of pictures of pretty girls which, he said, included beauty queens, night club singers and dancers and other assorted ladies of his acquaintance.

'These are just some of my girl friends,' he would announce proudly. 'I like girls who come from a working-class background, like myself. Factory girls, shop girls and typists. I get a kick out of taking ordinary girls to places they would not normally visit. I hate sophisticated women.'

It got so that Benny could virtually tailor his comments to suit the requirements of any particular publication. Thus it was that the writer from *Woman's Mirror* was able to leave with young Mr Hill's poetic account of a magic moment with a particular lady in his life: 'What with the wind blowing in her hair and her pretty summer frock, I very nearly asked her to marry me.'

Finding a wife for the bashful Mr Hill became a widespread preoccupation. Heather Jenner, wife of humorist Stephen Potter, included Benny on her guest list for a 1961 St Valentine's Day party at her London home to which she had invited 40 highly eligible women friends and 40 well-known bachelors.

'There are masses of bachelors about who should have a wife in their lives,' insisted Heather. 'I'm going to give a prize to the person giving me the best reason for remaining a bachelor or spinster.'

Benny, however, stayed away from this mating game. 'He says he is too much of a coward to come,' reported Heather.

But Benny continued to play the role of the free-wheeling bachelor with an eye for a pretty girl. His drawer full of pictures was almost overflowing.

'A lot of them are models,' he observed, riffling through a fistful of snapshots. 'One likes to wash my hair. I don't know why.'

Breezily, he informed one reporter: 'Look, if you should find yourself with a bit of spare, you know where I am. Or send them both around. I'll try to cope.'

Newspapers having branded him as a bachelor-at-large, Benny appeared happy to play along by projecting himself as a somewhat rakish gadabout with a constantly roving eye. Greeting callers at his Kensington flat in London, he would stand behind the door and inquire: 'Who's there? Is it somebody pretty, somebody nice?'

On a trip to make some appearances in Australia in 1960, he plotted a route which allowed him to spend a few days in places like Hong Kong, Bangkok and Tokyo. 'What do you think I am making all those stops for?' he asked, responding to questions from reporters at London Airport. 'All those beautiful girls, of course.'

As if sensing that an overweight comedian with a cherubic face might be somewhat miscast in this role of suave seducer, the shrewd Mr Hill took great care to intersperse his comments on the opposite sex with an occasional vignette of himself as a somewhat solitary soul who very seldom got the girl.

A well-remembered television commercial for Strand cigarettes in the 1960s featured a man in a trenchcoat lighting a cigarette as he strolled gloomily through a cloud of swirling fog. 'You're never alone with a Strand,' intoned the voice-over.

Returning from a trip to the Far East, Benny confessed: 'I think I must be the chap who inspired that advertisement — the original Lonely Man.

'Out East I stood a chance with the birds. Here in London I'm back in the old routine, standing in line for the girls at parties, always way behind the heart throb singers.

'I wish our girls were fascinated by funnymen, but they're not.'

This somewhat wistful portrait of the little clown

constantly being elbowed out by more macho men was one which Benny painted in almost every interview. Back from his Australian trip, he mused: 'You go on Bondi beach and the girls are so beautIful you could take the first dozen you meet and form a chorus line better than any you'd find in London. You think: "Ay, ay, I'm all right here."

'Then you go round the corner and meet a dozen of the most handsome men you've ever seen. The girls don't want to know little old Benny.'

Still, when people asked the thoughtful young comic for a view of the future he responded with a vision of bachelor Benny encircled by good-looking ladies. 'It's my secret dream to tour the South of France with a revue of les nues,' he told show business columnist Weston Taylor in 1962. 'Only six quid a week, I know. But think of it. Parties, drinks, les girls. Wonderful.'

Few people could dent this devil-may-care image, and even if they did the break-through was purely temporary. 'Oh, I get my sentimental moments, he confessed in one of his less guarded conversations. 'I go home and visit my brother and his family and I see him with his kids and I get all sloppy and think how nice it would be to have a little one of my own.

'But then again, on one of my mad Continental holidays I'm wandering along the jolly old plage with a gorgeous blonde near the old Med and I think: "Cor, you can keep that married lark."'

Prompted by persistent pressmen, marriage was a topic which cropped up in Benny's conversation with unfailing regularity. 'It's true I'm a single lad,' he told

Ken Bailey of *The People* in a 1969 interview. 'And sometimes I wonder where it's all leading.

'But show business marriages seem so dicey, don't they? No, I mean that.

'And I don't think I'm promiscuous at all, really I don't. In all my life I reckon I have only taken four ladies abroad. And I mean, well, when you do, by the second day or so you find yourself saying to her: "Why the hell don't you go home, love?"

'I mean, you set up a nice evening out and then on the way she wants to waste time window shopping all through Paris or somewhere.'

Suggestions that Benny might actually NEED a wife were shrugged off nonchalantly. 'I love looking after myself,' he insisted. 'I've got my friends, a TV set and a 14lb Stilton cheese. What more do I need?'

Such dismissive responses were of little comfort to Benny's mother, who would have dearly loved to see him marry. This anxiety was acknowledged by Benny himself when he revealed that his mother, now dead, was always avidly interested in the actresses who worked with him on his TV show.

'She would ask first whether the girl was married,' he said. 'No, I'd say. Then she would admire the fact that the actress was reasonably well built and say to my father: "That's the kind of girl I'd like for a daughter-in-law, isn't it?"

'Whenever a certain type worked with me on TV my mother always made the same comment. I told one actress she met with my mother's approval but then said: "The trouble is, I don't think you're big enough."

'You see, I came from a fat family. My sister, brother and father were all fat, which prompted my mother to pay her finest compliment when she said: "That's a BIG girl, Benny."'

Benny still chuckles at the recollection of the objections which his mother raised when he fell in love with a French girl in Paris. 'I wanted to marry her,' he says, 'but my mother put me off by saying how impractical it would be because she would never be able to order anything in British shops!'

A constant procession of pretty girls passes through the *Benny Hill Show*, and Benny is not averse to occasionally escorting one to dinner. But such encounters are conducted in a courtly, almost old-fashioned manner.

In the 1970s an attractive actress called Barbara Lindley who appeared on the show was surprised to find herself the focus of his attentions. She reported: 'He sends me red roses and he sends me cards now and again saying why don't I meet him for dinner — and love to my mother.'

To those who know him, such seemingly outdated propriety comes as no surprise. For while the on-screen antics in the *Benny Hill Show* may border on the raunchy, Benny views modern day promiscuity with a certain amount of alarm and a considerable amount of nostalgia for the decorous days of yesteryear.

'If you made a pass at a girl when I was a lad she would probably tell you she didn't believe in THAT sort of thing,' he reflects. 'Today she would say: "Don't be long, I've got a date at eight o'clock."'

Few ladies, it seems, had cause for complaint when

Benny came to call. Bob Monkhouse recalls how Benny once came to his house when he was living in St John's Wood and, after meeting Bob's attractive secretary, asked her out one evening. 'She said he was delightful and charming,' said Monkhouse. 'And he didn't make a pass.

Bob Monkhouse adds: 'Benny's relationships with girls have always been with younger women, not older, more demanding or more mature women who would expect more from him than perhaps he wishes to give another human being.'

With the British popular press obsessed by the private lives of television personalities, and regularly serviced by the kiss-and-tell revelations of disgruntled ex-lovers, wishful thinking news editors have eagerly awaited ammunition which allow them to dish the dirt on television's King Leer.

After more than 30 years, they are still waiting. Even the most scandal-hungry publications have seldom been able to come up with anything more outrageous than an occasional vague report that Mr Hill has been seen in an expensive restaurant dining discreetly with a good-looking woman.

The one exception was a story which appeared in the *News of The World* in October, 1985. 'I Was Benny Hill's Love Slave' screamed the stark headline. Below was a claim by a 35-year-old actress and model called Stefanie Martian that she had indulged in a bizarre relationship with Benny after they met when she was a 16-year-old virgin. According to Stefanie, Benny never attempted to make love to her. She explained: 'He said: "I'm going to show you how to please me."

And that's how it was for the next six years. I had to devote myself to him, while he never laid a finger on me.

'It was a totally one-sided relationship and for months — naive as I was — I was convinced that was what sex was all about.'

Such lurid allegations contrast sharply with the much more endearing picture painted by other women who know Benny well.

'Benny isn't the dirty old man people think, chasing after scantily clad girls,' says Sue Upton, one of the original Hill's Angels and one of Benny's few close friends.

'More often than not the girls are chasing him. He is the perfect gentleman when he dates his glamour girls. They all say so. He always walks on the road side of the pavement — that's the height of good manners.

'He likes his special girls to call him Uncle Ben, and he called me Mum after my children were born. I think Benny is a man of simple tastes. He is very, very rich — I don't think he knows how wealthy he is — but he's down to earth.

'He is really the nicest, sweetest Uncle Ben any girl could wish for.'

Benny dismisses suggestions that in real life he is anything like the leering, lustful, girl-chasing characters he portrays on his shows. 'If I went around performing like that I'd get arrested,' he protests.

And Sue Upton stresses: 'People should realise that even when he's on TV as lecherous Fred Scuttle he's just acting a part.

'You don't expect Anthony Perkins to go around

knifing people like he did in *Psycho*. So you wouldn't expect Benny to go round groping his Angels, would you?'

Sue has her own personal theory about why Benny has never married. 'He has always put his work first,' she says. 'So the ladies have had to take second place.

'I think Benny is too set in his ways as a happy bachelor to change now.'

Max Bygraves, who has known Benny for almost 40 years, contributes to the theory that Benny's career has left little room for personal relationships.

'That was the one thing he had over all of us when we were trying to make our way in show business,' suggests Max. 'He always had a clear concentration, never had to look after a family or worry about a wife and kids.

'He could devote himself full time to sitting down and writing his material, spending 16 hours a day on it if he wanted to.

'Being in variety was a bloody lonely life, and it was very easy to fall by the wayside if you didn't have the tenacity to stick at it. You had to go all over Britain, spending a week in those dirty old towns. It was only if you loved the business that you stuck at it. If something else lured you, or your family wanted you back, it put an end to it all.'

Benny himself acknowledges that his personal life has been sacrificed for the sake of stardom. 'I've known lots of girls who were fine for a while,' he says.

'But I think where marriage is concerned, you've got to decide which way you're going. I doubt that I could be the show business performer I am today if I were married.'

Just one year away from an old age pension, ladies still loom large in the life of television's sauciest bachelor. 'But it's unlikely, I think, that I'll ever marry,' he suggests. 'Unless it's in my old age, for companionship.'

Mrs Ivy Lillywhite, who has known Benny since he joined her Southampton concert party as a teenager, is convinced that Benny doesn't feel sad at remaining unmarried.

'I don't think it grieves him,' she said. 'I think he is quite contented.'

Then, with a shake of her head, she added: 'Anyway, I think it would have to be rather an unusual woman that would be able to live with him. He doesn't stop talking, and he is quite different from the ordinary run of men.'

CHAPTER
SEVEN

Showtime

Business is brisk at The Anglers and the waterside pub next to the Thames Television studios buzzes with excited chatter and the occasional burst of laughter.

'It's always like this before a *Benny Hill Show*,' explains one of the young barmen, rushed off his feet by the never-ending demand for drinks. 'People really seem to be in the mood to enjoy themselves.'

The bar is packed with Benny Hill fans, some of the fortunate 400 who have been sent tickets for the taping of a new show at the studios in Teddington. With Benny only doing about three programmes a year, the tickets are very hard to come by and even Thames Television staff can't get hold of them.

'We've been waiting more than a year and had more or less given up,' said Mrs Joan Cooper, from Billericay in Essex. 'I can't believe we're really here.'

Unrecognised by the jostling crowd, producer Dennis Kirkland stands at the bar, drinking half a pint of bitter and occasionally smiling as he overhears the eager fans laughingly recalling their favourite Benny Hill joke or re-capping on some sketch which has stuck in their memory.

There is more than an hour to go before the filming of the show begins, but already some guests are queueing outside the studios, anxious to ensure that they get a good seat. Some have arrived in a coach party, and they scramble from the bus with the giggling enthusiasm of day trippers to the seaside.

From the moment the fans step inside the studios, informality becomes the keynote of the evening. A priest in a long cassock and wide-brimmed hat suddenly appears near the entrance to Studio One, grinning mischievously as the visitors respectfully step aside to let him through. There's something familiar about the clergyman's face and they realise, too late, that it is veteran character actor Bob Todd dressed for one of the sketches in the show.

Studio One is like an aircraft hangar, a forest of lights hanging from the ceiling to illuminate a set which on one side is arranged as the interior of a nightclub and on the other is prepared for a domestic scene round a kitchen table.

The audience, many of them in a television studio for the first time, gaze around curiously as cameramen get in position and studio staff wearing earphones mutter into microphones to director Dennis Kirkland in the control room.

Benny Hill, who has arrived several hours earlier, is in the make-up room, receiving the finishing touches for his first role as gangster Brooklyn Benny in a roaring 'twenties number.

Like many comedy programmes, the *Benny Hill Show* employs a 'warm-up' man, a professional comedian whose job is to ensure that the audience are relaxed and ready to enjoy themselves.

'We like to get the audience involved, and feel they are part of the show,' explains Kirkland.

The warm-up man on this particularly Friday evening is Chris Carlsen, an amiable, curly-haired comic with an ingratiating line in friendly patter.

'Hands up those who have been in a studio before,' he demands. 'I see, just a few.

'Well, let's all get friendly, shall we? I want you to turn to the person next to you. Done that? Good. Now, look into their eyes. Ready? Okay, now say, very slowly. I LOVE YOU.'

The audience, many of them face to face with total strangers, are momentarily dumbfounded until compère Chris adds urgently: 'No, silly, I don't mean it. Just shake hands.'

The moment dissolves in relieved laughter, but it has established just the mood of mateyness which Kirkland is hoping for.

Banks of TV monitors hang above the heads of the audience. These are used to show the scenes which have already been filmed, mainly on location. What the studio guests see are the remaining sequences which will be filmed and edited in to the hour-long show.

'See these effects microphones?' asks Chris Carlsen, pointing upwards. 'They pick up every sound. So if anyone had beans for breakfast, remember that this show goes out to millions of people.'

It's a vulgar, corny and almost childish line, but the audience laps it up, as if anxious not to be caught straight-faced in this atmosphere of compulsive jollity.

Casually dressed in sweater and slacks, Chris leans forward confidentially and points a cautionary finger. 'Television audiences here at Thames are famous, you know,' he announces. 'So you have a lot to live up to. What we want you to do is go potty.'

The required pottiness quickly emerges when the comedian introduces director Dennis Kirkland ('he's a nutcase and he's a bit deaf, so you have to make a lot of noise').

Thus encouraged, the audience gives wispy-haired Kirkland the kind of welcome even a television super-star would find somewhat overwhelming.

But that's nothing compared to the ovation which erupts when Benny Hill himself walks on to the set, shyly blinking in the bright lights and already dressed for the first production number in gangster-style black shirt and white tie and a broad-brimmed fedora hat.

The warmth of the welcome is astonishing. It is more than 30 years since Benny Hill first brought his own show to British television, but the undeniable evidence of the man's enduring popularity can be judged by the reaction of this Thames Television audience who rise to their feet as if in some privileged presence.

Those who are expecting something saucy or even outrageous from King Leer receive quick confirma-tion that they have come to the right place. Benny and director Dennis Kirkland get together for a quick sketch in which Benny plays the part of a woman on a crowded train and Kirkland is supposed to be a young man standing behind her. Kirkland's hand creeps round to grasp one of Benny's breasts and Benny, in a high-pitched voice, demands: 'Young man, would you mind moving your hand?'

Kirkland begins moving his hand in a sensuous, fondling movement and Benny lifts his eyes to heaven in mock ecstasy. 'Mmmm, that's better,' he murmurs.

It's a sequence which would undoubtedly be considered too outrageous even for the *Benny Hill Show*, but as a cheeky contribution to the pre-programme warm-up it strikes just the right note of naughtiness and paves the way for Benny to plunge into a poem which immediately adds to an atmosphere which is strikingly reminiscent of the music-halls of yesteryear.

Impudent eyes darting everywhere, Benny recites:

'Have you seen the dirty old man as he wanders by in the street,

With a dirty old hat on his dirty old head,

And dirty old rags on his feet,

And we say that we care, but do we really care,

Should that lonely old man live or die?

In your heart of hearts, do you really care?

No?

Neither do I!'

There are even more echoes from the days of variety theatres when Benny does a stand-up routine which could almost have been borrowed from one of his own cheeky-chappie appearances as a bottom-of-the-bill comic.

'Ladies and gentlemen, it is 18 months since I did

a show here,' he announces, with a somewhat pained look on his chubby face. 'And you won't believe this, but there is still no light in the gents' loo.

'Can you imagine what it's like, going in there with a match in one hand ...'

Re-inforced by the raising of an inquisitive eyebrow, the line hangs in the air, and while waiting for the laugh which he knows will come, Benny seems to be almost talking to himself, adding something which the audience can't quite hear and is, anyway, inconsequential.

It's a timing trick which has not gone unnoticed by students of humour like comedian Bob Monkhouse.

'Benny will sometimes continue to speak after the joke,' explains Bob. 'It's a facet of the "I wanna tell you" approach — Bob Hope is one of the great exponents, and even the great Max Miller did it.

'Benny will do the outline and then continue talking sotto voce. He'll say "There was this bride and groom who had such an exhausting time on their wedding night that he couldn't stay awake for a second ... and I suppose it would have been difficult for him anyway..."

'I can remember in the early days Benny would do the joke and then allow his eyes to go out of focus, and a little smile would linger round his lips while perhaps he rubbed his hands together or tilted his head. And he would be having a private smile to himself, as if to say "that was a joke I just did", and the audience would be laughing at the joke as though they were part of a slight conspiracy.'

There is certainly no shortage of conspirators

among the studio audience who gleefully follow Benny's monologue about the shortcomings of the lavatories at Thames Television and his explanation of how he was instructed to keep the toilet door closed with his foot ('It must be the only loo in the world where the door opens outwards. I shall never be able to look Thora Hird in the face again').

Then it's time for another poem, this one about a short-sighted poet called Paul Finch whose typewriter has been repaired by an equally short-sighted mechanic who has somehow managed to muddle up the keys so that the letter 'P' is where the 'F' should be, and vice versa.

The confusion leads to the sad saga of Fatricia and Feter, The Pinal Foem of Faul Pinch:

'She held his hand as they were wed
In the chafel of St Faul's,
They honeymooned in Niagara,
And she held him by the palls.'

Beaming mischievously as the applause washes warmly over him beneath the bright lights of the studio, Benny extends the one-big-happy-family approach by somewhat plaintively soliciting the support of the audience for the show they are about to see.

'If you hear something funny, would you please laugh,' he implores. 'If you see something that you think ought to be funny, but isn't, would you please laugh anyway, otherwise we'll have to run it through the laughter machine and it never quite sounds the same.'

Such anxieties prove to be totally unfounded. As if resenting the very suggestion that their real, live mirth can be replaced by a laughter-making machine, the audience guffaws its way through the next two hours with an enthusiasm which envelops even the oldest and weakest of jokes.

As Brooklyn Benny, the New York gangster, the unstoppable Mr Hill rattles off one-liners with the machine-gun speed of a Mafia hit man.

'Look at big Julie over there. Three weeks ago he had a haemorrhoid transplant, and it rejected him.

'And what about Bugsie? He loaned a guy ten thousand dollars for plastic surgery. The guy skips town, and now Bugsie don't even know what he looks like.

'Then there's poor old Mike. Last week his father was in a fire. Was he badly burned? Listen, lady, they don't kid around at the crematorium.'

Throughout the entire two hours, Benny Hill is scarcely off the set, delivering fast-paced comedy songs without a hint of hesitation, bobbing up word-perfect as bunny girl or a befeathered budgerigar in a cage, fussily arranging props on a kitchen table for a domestic scene, reducing Bob Todd to helpless laughter when a sketch goes slightly wrong.

Those who came seeking vintage Benny did not leave disappointed. The highlight of the evening was an item, filmed on location, which contained all the essential ingredients of a Hill classic — dubious taste, shameless vulgarity, brilliant inventiveness and inspired clowning. Benny was The Halitosis Kid, a Wild West cowboy with the kind of bad breath capable of killing anything from a prairie cactus to a troublesome outlaw.

When Benny was in breathing distance, eagles

dropped stunned from the sky, horses keeled over in their harness, plants wilted and brave men fled.

People were still laughing over it as they crowded into The Anglers for a drink after the filming ended and the lights dimmed in Studio One.

Dennis Kirkland seemed surprised by a suggestion that the successful completion of another show which would be distributed world-wide to an audience of millions should be marked by some kind of celebration.

'Do Fords have a party on the assembly line every time they make a new motor car?' he inquired ingenuously.

There was hardly anyone around by the time a chubby figure clutching a plastic bag slipped out of the darkened studios, nodding goodnight to the uniformed doorman.

For Benny Hill, another day's work was done.

CHAPTER
EIGHT

The Bawdy Brit

Pandemonium reigned at the San Jose penitentiary in California.

A full-scale riot seemed imminent as rampaging prisoners burned bedding in their cells, stuffed rags down the toilets so the plumbing overflowed and hurled missiles from the cell block windows.

In scenes reminiscent of an old James Cagney jailbreak movie, tin cups were rattled noisily across the iron bars of the cell doors and the prison echoed to a persistent chant from the angry inmates: 'We want Benny! We want Benny!'

Order was only restored when prison officials gave in to the convicts' desperate demand: permission to watch Benny Hill on TV.

The protest in the penitentiary, in April, 1982, began after the governor brought 'lights out' forward half an hour when he noticed that prisoners were turning up looking baggy-eyed at morning court appearances because they had stayed up late in the jail watching television.

What he hadn't realised was that the new 11.30 pm shut down would prevent the prison population watching their favourite TV programme, the *Benny Hill Show*.

In a way the incident was an appropriate accolade for the British comedian who has run riot on American television and achieved a popularity which some claim surpasses even that of his comic compatriot, Charlie Chaplin.

'The last outpost of naughtiness,' is how Robert MacKenzie of America's *TV Guide* describes the show. It's an outpost which the cheeky 'Limey' continues to defend with an armoury of sly gags, saucy sketches and the kind of raunchy repertoire which still occasionally prompts maiden aunts in the midwest to reach for the telephone and register spinsterly complaints with their local TV station.

'The funny thing is, they never seem to call up when the show is actually on the air,' observed one Chicago television executive. 'They always watch the programme through to the end, in case it gets even more shocking.'

Almost 10 years after it was first seen in the United States, the *Benny Hill Show* is still holding down large audiences from coast to coast. It is seen in 80 cities, from Anchorage to Atlanta. Because of the limited number of shows available for screening, some stations are on their fourth or fifth re-run of the same programmes.

But there are few complaints from viewers who

seem to find something new to laugh at even the fifth time around. Howard Rosenberg of the *Los Angeles Times* concludes: '*The Benny Hill Show* is a glittering, gaudy bauble that independent stations — always ravenous for fresh products with which to compete with network stations — can deploy as a comedy of their own. And one that is titillating, at that.'

The fact that the *Benny Hill Show* is screened largely by local independent stations rather than the major American networks such as NBC or CBS has been the key to its success in the USA.

But the popularity of the programme also owes much to the shrewdness and tenacity of the man who masterminded the marketing of the programme in the States, Don Taffner.

Taffner, a cheerful, dapper Brooklyn-born American with a liking for colourful shirts, started out in show business as a messenger boy for the William Morris Agency in New York more than 35 years ago. Today he heads D. L. Taffner Ltd, an international marketing, production and distribution company with offices in America, Great Britain, Canada, Ireland and Australia which handles TV and video programmes ranging from *Danger Mouse* to *Edward and Mrs Simpson*.

The launching pad for the *Benny Hill Show* was a suite high up in the impressive, round-towered Bonaventure Hotel in downtown Los Angeles. It was there, on a gale-lashed California day in 1978, that Don Taffner stood looking out of the window at the torrential rain which was so heavy that it was leaking into the spectacular glass elevators which run up the outside of the building and soaking the hapless occupants.

The absence of the famous California sunshine bothered Don not at all. In fact, the harder it rained, the better he liked it. For the hotel was full of delegates to the convention of the National Association of Television Programme Executives (NATPE), and the bespectacled New York agent realised that the foul weather was likely to keep most of the conventioneers inside the Bonaventure.

And, as a salesman, that suited him fine. It provided him with a captive audience for a new programme which he was eager to screen for the scores of buyers from television stations all over the country who were at the NATPE get-together looking for fresh material. The buyers had never heard of the programme which Taffner was pushing, but he planned to change that situation by screening for their benefit a 30 minute tape featuring an unknown British comic who dressed up in funny clothes and surrounded himself with pretty girls.

It was called the *Benny Hill Show*.

As an agent for Thames Television, Don himself was no stranger to Benny Hill. 'I thought he was a really funny little guy, and I had an idea that the American public would like him too, if only they got the chance to see him,' explained Taffner.

But there were major obstacles to be overcome in getting Benny on to American TV screens. Although it was possible to sell major documentaries like impressive *World At War* series there was an in-built opposition to British comedy from those who thought that the United Kingdom's sense of humour just wouldn't be appreciated in the USA.

Some even complained that they couldn't understand the British accent, an objection which caused Don Taffner much frustration. 'I have never understood Marlon Brando in my entire life,' he would argue. 'But that didn't stop him becoming an international star.'

Said Don: 'I knew that if we could get past the station bosses and the programme managers and actually get Benny in front of the public, we would be in pretty good shape.'

The other big snag was the hour-long format of the show, which did not sit comfortably with American television schedules where most comedy programmes ran for only 30 minutes (less numerous commercial breaks).

Keen to overcome these problems, Taffner contacted Philip Jones, the head of Thames Television light entertainment division in London. It was decided to experiment by editing some of the existing Benny Hill shows into a tight, fast moving 30-minute segment, stripped of British gags which were so localised that they would have little meaning in the States.

It was this tape which Taffner screened for the buyers at the Bonaventure Hotel in Los Angeles. 'I introduced the show by telling them that Benny Hill had been a phenomenon on TV in Britain and abroad for many years,' he explained. 'But really I let the show speak for itself.'

Such simple strategy paid off handsomely. From the moment Benny's face peered out at them through his Fred Scuttle glasses, the hardened buyers began chuckling. Then, as Benny and his girls romped through the racy routines already so familiar to British audiences, the tough TV men began to collapse with laughter, some dabbing at their eyes with handkerchiefs.

Despite this apparent enthusiasm, Don Taffner didn't reach for the celebration champagne. 'I'd seen it before,' he said. 'Buyers would laugh like hell for half an hour and then turn round and say: "But we can't buy it — it's British."'

Indeed, nobody actually bought the *Benny Hill Show* at the Bonaventure Hotel. But it had been a promising start. Taffner was convinced that if he could persuade six or seven independent stations to take the show, it would justify the expense of going into full scale production with as many of the half hour edited shows as Thames could produce.

From his offices in New York, Los Angeles, Atlanta and Chicago, Taffner's salesmen followed up on the convention presentation, calling on TV stations and showing them the Benny Hill tape, urging station managers to let their viewers at least sample the talents of the unknown, chubby-faced comic from the other side of the Atlantic.

It was a hard sell, but it worked. In January, 1979, independent stations in four major cities signed to take the show — WPBT in Miami, WTAF in Philadelphia, KVOS in Seattle/Tacoma and WUAB in Cleveland.

In Philadelphia in particular the show was an instant hit, soaring up the ratings. 'Overnight it was the talk of the town,' recalls Vince DeNoble, film supervisor at WTAF. 'It was different, that's for sure, and we certainly didn't have anything like it in the States.

'I remember a lot of guys here at the station looking at it and saying: "Wow! We're gonna air THIS?" But our buyers had seen the show, liked it, and were convinced that it would go.'

And go it did, in the city of brotherly love. 'Philadelphia is a fairly conservative city, and I think people were a little startled by the *Benny Hill Show* at first,' said Lee Winfrey, TV critic of the *Philadelphia Inquirer*. 'It was a little bawdy for local television

'But it was novel, and refreshing, and I don't think English music-hall humour had ever been seen here before. People were amused and charmed by it.'

The Philadelphia success story quickly spread. Other big cities scrambled for the programme, and in a matter of months it was being screened by WOR in New York, WLVI in Boston, KERA in Dallas, KCOP in Los Angeles, KTVU in San Francisco and WDCA in Washington DC.

New Yorkers went so crazy over Benny Hill that WOR, which had previously been best known for its sports coverage, was forced to put it on twice a night. Even their popular *Bowling For Dollars* programme was pushed aside to make way for Benny.

Matched against *All In The Family* and *M*A*S*H* on New York's rival Channel 5, the *Benny Hill Show* more than held its own. Channel 5 executives were reported to be livid with the success of Benny' s programme, not least because the two *Benny Hill Shows* cost just $5,000 to put on while *All In The Family* and *M*A*S*H* cost three times that amount.

'What's the most outrageous show on television?'

asked George Maskian in the *New York Daily News*. 'If you think it's *The Gong Show* then obviously you've never watched Benny Hill, king of double entendres, on Channel 9. Hill is Britain's most popular comedian, and he's gaining on these shores as well.

'Since the series started here last April, the ratings have skyrocketed, making it the highest rated show on the station. It also tops all the independents in the week night 11 pm period.

'Channel 9 says it gets more complimentary mail than protests about the overtly sexy material presented on the series. "It's sexy but not offensive," said a station spokesman. "It beats *Monty Python* coming and going.

Suddenly, America just couldn't get enough of Benny Hill — and that posed yet another problem for Don Taffner and Thames. Some stations followed the lead of WOR in New York and began showing the programme every week night from Monday to Friday, a practice professionally known as 'stripping'. Gratifying though this was for Taffner and Thames, it meant that the available programmes were being gobbled up at an alarming rate.

In London, Philip Jones of Thames called in John Street, one of Benny's former producers at the BBC, and set him to work editing 38 hours of old Benny Hill material to create new shows for the USA.

On the face of it, such a stockpile should have instantly produced almost eighty half-hour shows for the American market. Allowing for commercials, the shows were running for $22^1/_2$ minutes in America. But the editing of the British-made shows in order to produce a fast-paced package for US audiences meant that sketches which had run for two minutes in the original version would be cut to seconds in the States. Guest artistes who would be unknown in America were scissored out, as were jokes that were just too British for American viewers to understand.

'In the States we like a lot of action on screen, with plenty of things happening,' explains Don Taffner. 'By editing out various items, we were left with a very fast half hour of pure Benny Hill. And that's just what the viewers wanted.

'The fact that the shows were put together from various programmes which had been produced over a number of years meant that sometimes Benny seemed to change in appearance from sketch to sketch — suddenly he would look a lot younger if the sequence was from one of his early shows, or you would notice that he had put on a little weight in another segment. But that didn't matter. It was all Benny Hill, and that's what counted.'

Working flat out to cope with the demand, Thames put together 40 half-hour shows, which were eagerly snapped up by independent stations anxious to cash in on the Benny boom. Some ran two of them a night, showing them all over again when they reached the end of their supply.

'Benny Hill shows are like oil, a rare resource that will run out one day,' said Pat Argue of WOR in New York. 'Benny Hill is a genius. It's as simple as that. I'm an ardent feminist, but apart from the odd rape joke I don't get upset about his show. He's vulgar on such an absolutely universal human level.'

While Benny might have been popular with the public, he certainly wasn't popular with bar owners in some towns who complained that their regular customers were staying home to watch the Benny Hill show five nights a week.

Henry McGee, one of the regulars on the show, discovered on a holiday in America that one New York discotheque had solved this problem in a most enterprising manner. 'They suddenly stopped the dancing, wheeled on two huge television sets, and onto the screen came Benny,' said Henry. 'Everybody laughed themselves silly. Then the show ended, the sets were wheeled away and the disco restarted.'

America seemed insatiable in its demand for the shows, but Benny and Thames resisted all efforts to produce new shows tailor-made for the burgeoning American market.

'We're reluctant to see Benny change his style of show,' explained Philip Jones of Thames. 'We just don't want him to become mid-Atlantic, part American and part the very British comic he is.'

In fact, it was the unique 'Britishness' of Benny's shows which seemed to appeal to Americans who had never before been exposed to such naughtiness in prime time. Under the headline 'Benny, The Bawdy Brit', Susan Sawyer wrote in the *New York Daily News*: 'Benny Hill would seem an unlikely candidate for American cult hero. But Brits have been laughing at him for years. And though some people call his humour sexist, others just plain bad taste, even in America, Hill is fast becoming a comic legend.

'Locally, segments from his last 10 years' work are

aired on Channel 9 weeknights at 11 pm, drawing the Mary Hartman crowd and resurrecting sniggers not heard since the prime time of Red Skelton.'

As the number of stations screening Benny Hill across America rose to 25, Michael Billington in the *New York Times* set out to analyse the secret of Benny's success.

'Watching Mr Hill's shows is a bit like being hit over the head with a stack of saucy seaside postcards,' wrote Mr Billington. 'His popularity on American television is probably the most unexpected conquest of the continent since the Pilgrims landed on Plymouth Rock.

Benny himself told the *New York Times* writer: 'I never set out to capture any specific audience. I've never thought this bit is for a little old lady in Glasgow, or even Duluth.

'The mistake British comedians often make is trying to beat the Americans at their own game — getting visiting American singers on their shows, talking about sidewalk instead of pavement, sitting on high stools in a white dinner jacket doing ballads. That way you end up with a mid-Atlantic mish-mash. What we've discovered is that Americans seem to love our saucy humour.'

Don Taffner's strategy of side-stepping the national networks and selling direct to local stations was paying off handsomely. A side benefit was the fact that, because the show was not networked across the country, it was not reviewed simultaneously by TV critics in the big city newspapers. The public were able to judge the show for themselves.

'That suited the direction we were going,' said Don Taffner. 'Once the public likes it, the critics will like it.'

How right he was. When the show was first screened by WOR in New York, it was the subject of a scathing attack by James Wolcott in the weekly newspaper *Village Voice*. Eight months later, having captured the hearts and minds of American viewers, Benny had also managed to charm the previously unimpressed Mr Wolcott.

Writing in The Village Voice of 7 January, 1980, a penitent Wolcott admitted: 'The surprise triumph of the 1979 television season has been the unblushing, bawdy, *Benny Hill Show*.

'When Benny Hill premiered last spring, I threw a Calvinistic tantrum, damning the show for its porno-graphic grubbiness. Voice readers flipped the page in forgiving silence, knowing that I would eventually come to my senses, and I have. For despite all the dips and bumps, the *Benny Hill Show* is an exhilaratingly smutty spree — the funniest gift the British have dropped on our laps since Bea Lillie.

'It's Benny Hill's pornographic grubbiness that makes him so special, so subversively sane. He's a music-hall lech, with a jovial belly, porky eyes and cheeks so plump and shiny they look like unnippled breasts.'

Many critics were obviously bemused by Benny. They had never seen anything quite like him before, romping gleefully across their screens with a spicy mixture of material which came as something of a shock to a nation whose prudish television watchdogs wouldn't even allow brassiere manufacturers to use human models in their TV commercials.

Howard Rosenberg of the *Los Angeles Times* gave voice to this confusion when he called the *Benny Hill Show* 'a sort of polished drivel, a triumph of trash so revolting that, unbelievably, you tend to like it.'

If the critics were confused, the public certainly weren't. Benny Hill mania was abroad, and there wasn't an apartment house doorman in Manhattan who couldn't do a creditable Fred Scuttle impersonation, peaked hat askew, tongue poking out and fingers splayed in a sloppy salute.

Waiters at the Algonquin Hotel in New York did lightning Benny Hill impressions, and policemen guarding Cuban leader Fidel Castro on a visit to the United Nations headquarters were glimpsed scurrying along First Avenue with night sticks held aloft, aping a Keystone Kops sequence seen the night before in the *Benny Hill Show*.

In New York, agent Don Taffner's office was kept busy forwarding fan mail to Benny in England. One was from a spinster in Texas who wrote: 'Dear Benny, I love your show, but my mother is a straight-laced Catholic woman and she says she doesn't like it. However, now and then I catch her peeking over the top of her newspaper at it.'

There was hardly a city in the United States which wasn't running the *Benny Hill Show* at some time of the day or night, and it was estimated that a quarter of all the TV sets in America were tuned in to his outrageous antics.

In Los Angeles, KCOP television were running the show twice a night, at 6.30 and 11 pm, and *Los Ange-*

les Times critic Lawrence Christon reported: 'No other comedy show uses television as a visual medium as well as the *Benny Hill Show*. It's brightly lit, with a relatively uncluttered look, and he often takes us outdoors.

'At its heart, though, is Hill's expert comedic sense. The crispness of his attack distracts us from threadbare toilet references, and the smirky benignity of his personality lets him slip into many more comic guises than we might tolerate from someone else.

'No television show since *Laugh-in* has used cutting and rhythm to such comic ends.' It was at KCOP that the switchboard lit up after one particular *Benny Hill Show* featured a saucier than usual scene which had somehow slipped by the censor. Filmed in Australia, the sequence showed three very well-endowed topless ladies taking a shower in a makeshift outback shack, with a leering Benny beating the flowered pattern off a rug hanging over a line as he watched.

The station was inundated with telephone calls. A few were from viewers who had been shocked by the nudity. But hundreds more were from people who had missed the show, been told about it by friends, and were now insisting that the sequence should be shown all over again.

'We usually check new episodes carefully, but this one got through,' said programming director Peter Schlesinger.

Meanwhile, Howard Rosenberg, also of the Los Angeles Times, was finally overcoming his previous bewilderment and coming to some new conclusions about the reasons for the show's phenomenal success.

'Americans obviously see more in the *Benny Hill Show* than nostalgia,' he wrote, in April 1980. 'There is also more to Benny Hill than his ability to provoke laughter by tackling the absurd, his capacity to remain somehow essentially likeable while at the same time being offensive.

'Sex — yes, even cheap Benny Hill-type sex — has universal appeal. That, more than anything, is probably why the *Benny Hill Show* is astoundingly successful on so many US stations. Though hardly explicit by current standards, the *Benny Hill Show* is probably the most ribald happening on US television.'

It was inevitable that such ribaldry would not meet with universal approval. The sight of lusty old men removing their trousers to chase scantily clad girls across a field led to telephoned objections from some New York viewers. And there were cries of 'racism' when, in a take-off of *Gone With the Wind*, Bob Todd played a black southern servant with rolling eyes while Benny preened in a crinoline as a blushing southern belle.

In Miami, where the programme went on five nights a week at 7 pm, a group of concerned teachers and parents organised a petition demanding that the *Benny Hill Show* should only be screened after children were in bed. They said the girls were too scantily clad, and claimed that boys as young as seven had been pinching girls' bottoms in playground imitations of Benny.

But such objections did nothing to halt the mounting popularity of the twinkling-eyed Englishman whose shows were getting better ratings than the eve-

ning news programmes in some cities. Even the re-
peats pulled in viewers by the million.

'That's what surprised me, the evergreen attitude to
the shows,' says agent Don Taffner. 'Try to analyse
why a *Benny Hill Show* is as watchable in its 15th run
as it is in its first, and you start thinking in terms of
animated shows for children. In a sense, Benny's
sketches are animated shows for adults. I have been to
cocktail parties with doctors and professors who talk
about the sketches the same way that children talk
about Donald Duck.'

It was Taffner who first sensed that the universal
appeal of Benny's approach could break down the
barriers which traditionally had kept non-American
comics from appearing on TV in the United States.

'In the early days of TV in the States we had visual
comics, and of course they got maximum exposure
and eventually some of them became just too familiar,' he explained, relaxing in his elegant Manhattan
office.

'Then along comes Benny. In a way he belongs to
the past, a reminder of the Three Stooges and that
kind of thing. Yet, at the same time, to an American
audience he is new — a funny little guy, a great comedian they haven't seen before.

'It's as if Abbott and Costello suddenly showed up
in Britain and you'd never seen them before.'

The emergence of this previously unknown comic
genius intrigued Americans, and the London corre-
spondents of US newspapers and magazines were
kept busy filing profiles about the career of the shy
funnyman who had started his working life as a milk-

man and ended up as one of the best-known television personalities in the States. They called him 'Britain's naughty court jester' and the headlines trumpeted: 'All Hail King Leer.'

Anthony Slide of *Gallery* magazine wanted to know why Benny's British-oriented show had made such great inroads in the USA.

'I haven't an idea, I haven't a clue,' Benny told him. 'In the past I've done one or two Anglo-American shows, on which there's been an American producer, and there's been quite a bit of "they won't like that" or "they wouldn't understand that" instead of writing and doing what you want to.

'You try to please the American producer and his interpretation of what the people like over there, and one misses out that way.

'My show goes to a lot of countries and you can't shoot it for France, for Germany or for Greece. If it's been successful this way, leave it like that.

'In point of fact I did think it would be a good idea to get American guest singers for the show. But then if the singer is living in America and can go on television any time he likes, there's no great advantage to having him come over here and sing.'

America's curiosity about Benny Hill was heightened by the fact that Benny had never actually been to the United States. His London agent, Richard Stone, was inundated with requests for Benny to make television shows in the USA or appear live in cabaret. Casinos in Las Vegas, Reno and Atlantic City offered him up to $1,000,000 to appear in stage shows, but all such approaches were politely but firmly rejected by

Benny himself.

'I keep getting million-dollar offers to do things that are not up my street,' said Benny. 'American TV could probably offer 39 shows a year, but you have to read your lines off cards and you have no control over who's writing the scripts.

'Can you see me coming down that studio staircase, with girls dressed as Beefeaters on either side, pretending to introduce guests? The American gentlemen are being very kind and all that. But it's just a matter of keeping a *Benny Hill Show* a real *Benny Hill Show*. I'm happy as I am, doing three shows a year for Thames.

The glitter of Las Vegas and the bright lights of Broadway got equally short shrift. 'It is Bruce Forsyth's dearest wish to conquer Broadway,' observed Benny. 'I wouldn't give you tuppence to go to Broadway.

'I don't do live shows, and I'd be lost on a cabaret floor, million dollars or not.'

Benny's sentiments were echoed by producer Dennis Kirkland, who added: 'We shoot for Britain. It's the only way we know, and the only way we want to know. There have been suggestions that Benny should go and work in the States, but he isn't interested. He doesn't want to lumber himself with 30 script writers and 10 script editors. He'd rather carry on as he does now, with just the two of us working out the shows.'

An important part of the show's success in the States lay with what television marketing men in America call 'the jiggle factor' — the sexy element, supplied in this case by the raunchy Hill's Angels. The jiggle factor progressed a point or two when the *Benny*

Hill Show was sold to cable TV organisations such as Home Box Office.

'For a variety of reasons there is a different sense of expectation one receives from a free service and that of a pay TV service,' explained Richard Gitter of the NBC network's Office of Broadcast Standards. 'The very same viewers who have sexually explicit options on their pay tier will be the very same to argue or yell foul if such a product is aired on the networks. I suppose that if one is paying money for a programme, one's expectations will be different.'

Roughly translated, that means that subscribers to cable television can expect to see much steamier stuff. So it was that Home Box Office enticingly announced its latest acquisition: 'More All-New Unexpurgated Benny Hill.'

'Some may wonder how this show could possibly get more explicit without tumbling into outright pornography,' wrote *New York Times* TV critic John J. O'Connor. 'But the greater freedom of cable adds up to little more than a heavier emphasis on female breasts, many of them topless, and posteriors, arranged whenever possible for maximum exposure. These are supplied by a bevy of attractive women called Hill's Angels.

'The Benny Hill experience can be described as a vaudeville-burlesque roller coaster. The pacing is frantic as sketches, skits and sight gags spill over each other, some hilarious, others merely silly. At the centre nearly always is Mr Hill, who in response could be mistaken for a rather pudgy, middle-aged shoe clerk.

'But then he's rarely in repose as he jumps in and

out of costumes, many of them, in the time-honoured British tradition, being women's dresses.

'The Hill's Angels are rarely out of camera range, smilingly wriggling, bumping and grinding — much to the unabashed delight of Mr Hill and, evidently, his audiences.'

Such salacious goings-on were also warmly welcomed by Marvin Kitman, television critic of *Newsday*. 'Let me warn any desperate people looking for a laugh that The Unexpurgated Benny Hill is off-colour, as the British say,' wrote Kitman.

'It's smutty, bawdy, raunchy, tasteless, disgusting, evil. In other words, right down my gutter.

'This is the kind of programme that will give the Moral Majority a stroke. The kind of filth in Benny Hill is probably bad for my soul. Well, luvs, he's funny, and I don't care if I fry in hell for thinking so.

'The humour, at its best, is on the level of the bawdy postcards they used to sell at souvenir shops in Brighton and Blackpool. The ones parents used to try to prevent their children from looking at sideways, lest they be corrupted.

'I've never been to any of those English beach resorts, and I still think it's amusing. It just goes to show that this kind of humour must travel better than British wines.

'I see Benny Hill as the English Bob Hope. Hope looks as if he is one of Hill's cousins, one of his English relatives. Take a look at his face. Hill is what Hope would have been if he had stayed in England, instead of coming to Cleveland.'

By 1984, the *Benny Hill Show* was being seen on

more than 100 outlets right across the United States. The American sales, estimated at $10 million, helped Thames Television win The Queen's Award For Export Achievement.

'In a way, the fact that Benny had never actually been to America somehow added to the mystique of the man,' suggested agent Don Taffner. 'Almost every day we were getting requests for him to perform in the States, do a show in Vegas or appear on Broadway. But he resisted them all.'

Eventually the Mafia put a price on Benny's head. This came to light when a Thames Television crew were in the United States, making a series about the Cosa Nostra called *Crime Inc*. They were filming an interview with a 'businessman' who was suspected of being a highly placed mobster with one of the Mafia 'families' when he became very upset over questions linking one of his gambling casinos with organised crime. He stormed away from the interviewer, refusing to answer any more questions.

Cameraman Ted Adcock chased after him, pleading with the Mafia man to complete the interview. A heated discussion ensued until the crime boss suddenly paused and looked inquisitively at the British cameraman.

'Hey, listen,' he said. 'Do you know Benny Hill?'

Surprised, and somewhat puzzled, Adcock replied: 'Yes. As a matter of fact, I've worked on some of his shows.'

Glancing around warily, as if anxious to make sure they were not being watched, the mobster put his arm round Adcock's shoulder and led him into a quiet corner.

'Look,' said the crime boss. 'I'm gonna make a deal with you. I'll come back and finish the interview, but you gotta promise to get a message to Benny Hill for me. Tell him I want him to do a show at my casino. Tell him not to worry about the money — he can name his own price. We gotta deal?'

Adcock gulped and took the mobster's outstretched hand. 'Er … I'll do my best,' he said.

'Okay,' said the Mafia man. 'Now, let's finish that interview.'

And so the Thames cameraman flew back to Britain to deliver to Benny Bill what might well be considered the ultimate invitation — an offer he couldn't refuse.

CHAPTER
NINE

Mr Lonely

It was Christmas day, but there was little seasonal cheer in the home of the millionaire comedian with one of the best known faces in the world.

Like some latter-day Scrooge, Benny Hill sat alone and shivering in an unheated house, watching television.

On a table in the icy kitchen stood the remains of his Christmas dinner — sausage and mash. The floor was covered with buckets and bowls of water. Bitterly cold weather had frozen the pipes of the modest semi-detached house in Westrow Gardens, Southampton, and Benny had been forced to fetch water from the homes of neighbours.

He had shaved that Christmas morning in 1986 in the same water he used to boil his breakfast egg.

Fairy lights twinkled in the windows of other houses in the quiet cul-de-sac and sounds of merriment could be heard as families pulled crackers and donned paper hats while eating the traditional turkey and Christmas pudding.

There were no such festivities at the Hill home, where Benny sat watching the *Lenny Henry Show* on TV. Occasionally he took a sip from a small glass of Chartreuse liqueur, his only concession to the seasonal celebrations.

'He could have gone anywhere in the world for Christmas — the Bahamas, the West Indies, anywhere,' says Mrs Alice Moore, a neighbour who has known him for more than 50 years. 'But he preferred to be on his own, in the house where he grew up.

'The pipes in his house were frozen, so he would pop in now and then for another bucket of water.

'We didn't like to think of him being on his own, and my sister took him a little bottle of Chartreuse and a piece of Christmas pudding with a couple of mince pies.

'But he said he was perfectly happy and told us not to worry about him. He had his TV for company, and he was quite content.'

To an outsider, the idea of a wealthy and famous entertainer like Benny Hill spending Christmas in the reclusive style of a Howard Hughes may seem strange. Such apparent eccentricity, however, comes as no surprise to those who know him best.

'He may be surrounded by all those gorgeous girls on TV,' suggested Mrs Moore. 'But in reality, he's a loner.'

Because he lives modestly, shuns the glitter of show business and is seldom seen at star-studded social occasions, some observers have chosen to portray

Benny as an enigmatic character whose desire for privacy is nothing more than a defensive ploy to hide some deeply hidden unhappiness.

But Dennis Kirkland, the producer of his TV show and probably his closest friend, insists that such deductions are totally inaccurate.

'Because he is such a big star, some people seem disappointed that he is not flash or flamboyant,' says Dennis. 'The truth is that he is a very ordinary bloke with very ordinary tastes.

'He likes spicy, eastern food and will sometimes eat in the Royal Garden Hotel in Kensington. But he is just as happy coming to stay with me and nipping down the local Indian tandoori restaurant.

'He doesn't like to go into places where he will be recognised, although he doesn't mind signing autographs.'

Although he is unfailingly polite to fans who recognise him, Benny harbours a reluctance to get too involved with the public which dates back to his early success.

'When I used to do big summer seasons, people would grab me on the promenade for a photograph with their baby,' he explains. 'They never asked. I was just their property. I didn't feel like a human being.'

His avoidance of parties has similar origins. All too often in the past an invitation has turned out to be nothing more than an opportunity for the host or hostess to put Benny on show to the guests, a situation in which he has resented the idea of having to 'sing for his supper'.

'I become more anti-social as the years go by,'

Benny admits. 'I try to avoid parties because I know I won't enjoy myself.

'Sometimes I've been conned by promises of scores of lovely ladies. But I always end up in a corner clutching a light ale and listening to someone's bank manager telling me a funny joke.

'I've been caught so many times that these days I'd rather stay home with my telly and a plate of fish fingers.'

For the shy entertainer, nothing is more embarrassing or annoying than suddenly becoming the centre of attraction when he is relaxing on an evening out.

To his dismay, he was recognised by the ringmaster while watching a circus in Amsterdam. The spotlight was trained on him, and the entire audience strained for a glimpse of the man they had seen so often on their TV sets. 'I felt like a performing elephant,' says Benny.

And he fled in terror when a stripper in a Hamburg night club, prowling the audience for a 'volunteer' to join in her act, suddenly stopped in front of Benny and asked: 'Don't I know you from somewhere?'

Such experiences are all the more exasperating because Benny deliberately chooses to go abroad for his holidays to avoid the kind of public adulation he would receive if he turned up on vacation at a British seaside resort.

His trips abroad are often spur-of-the-moment decisions which see him departing for the airport with a small suitcase containing little more than a toothbrush and spare underwear. He seldom takes even a fresh shirt, preferring to buy new ones as and when he needs them.

He loves the Continent, and regularly visits Barcelona, Madrid, Paris, Marseilles, Amsterdam and Hamburg, almost invariably alone. It's a wanderlust which originated during his time in the Army in World War Two.

'I was sent to Normandy,' he recalls, 'and when I got inland a bit and clapped eyes on a typical French street with pavement cafés, gendarmes and blokes in berets — well, despite the shells and bullets and things, that was it. I was hooked on the travel lark.

'I've been all round the world, but I've now settled for one or two really favourite haunts to revisit each year, and they all happen to be in Europe.

'Take Marseilles, for instance. I'd always been fascinated by the place long before I went there. Then when I finally got there, I had this wonderful feeling. Something inside me said: "You're home, Benny boy."'

Although he could easily afford to stay at the best hotels, with high-speed laundry services available at the push of a button, the years he spend surviving in dingy 'digs' while playing the provincial music-halls have made him very self-sufficient. 'The first thing I do when I arrive at a hotel is to take off my socks, wash them and hang them up,' he says.

'And I discovered early on that if you washed out a shirt and draped the right bits over a mirror or glass-topped dressing-table they would dry as stiff as a board.

'I buy most of my shirts abroad. I go away in one that's nearly dead and take another one with me. Then

I'll nip out and buy two or three new ones. When I come home I roll them up and throw them away in the waste-paper basket.'

Paris has long been one of his favourite destinations, though the success of the *Benny Hill Show* on French television has made it more and more difficult to remain unrecognised as he sits at one of the pavement cafés, surveying a passing scene which is often the inspiration for script ideas. The clumsy waiter who spills the pastis is almost certain to figure in a Benny Hill sketch at some future date.

Benny's choice of hotels is as unpredictable as his travel plans. He might spend one night in the opulence of the famous George V, only to check out and spend the next few nights in a £25 a night side-street hotel in Montmartre.

In Marseilles you are likely to find him whiling away a couple of hours in a nondescript Arab cinema or studying the local paper for Saints' day festivals to which he travels by bus.

He's something of a football fan, and often if he is in a city like Madrid or Munich he will join the crowd at a local match.

On other occasions he will head for the Carmargue region, where horses and bulls are bred. He is at his happiest staying incognito in some small village guest-house, sampling the local wine and walking through the hillsides.

'I am a happy sort of soul,' he insists. 'I don't go through life shouting for the waiter.'

Whatever Benny gets up to on these jaunts abroad, it is obviously not restricted to soccer, sightseeing and

Saints' days. 'I once had a weekend in Hamburg I'll never forget,' he recalls. 'And there was a week in Bangkok that will take a bit of forgetting, too.

'I investigated some of those bath houses and disco bars where they have little girls in bikinis. It was all very sad. I ended up buying everyone in the bar a drink to cheer them up.

'One by one they all lined up to kiss me goodbye, even the managers and the bouncers. I was covered in every shade of lipstick.'

Although Benny has been known to occasionally take a lady companion on holiday, he is more often than not alone. 'I am basically a loner,' he explains. 'I'm awfully self-sufficient. Very rarely do I need somebody.'

The fact that Benny has so much free time in which to travel stems from his insistence on doing only three or four television shows a year. Outside his own programmes he is seldom seen on TV and a live stage appearance is a rarity.

'I won't do a live stage show for anything,' he says. 'Promoters never stop asking me to go on stage. They say I could make millions.

'But they've all forgotten that life is for living, not slaving. I want my nights free. Stuck in a blinkin' theatre every night isn't for me.

'I never liked being on stage. It's no joy on a November evening, when it's raining outside, to have to get up and go to a draughty theatre to do two houses when you know the first one is going to be empty and the second one isn't going to be much better.

'And you never know when you are going to get

drunks in who will give you a hard time, and you can't cut and go back and do it again like you can in a TV show.'

Though it is understandable that Benny should retain such gloomy recollections of his days in the provincial music-hall, his firmly established place as one of Britain's favourite comedians would almost certainly ensure packed houses should he ever choose to return to the stage. But that's unlikely.

'I think I fulfil my obligation to the public with what I have already undertaken,' he says.

Although Benny still harbours bitter memories of the night he 'got the bird' from the audience at Sunderland Empire when he was an aspiring young comedian in variety, this reluctance to do live stage shows has nothing to do with a lack of confidence or inability to put comedy across in a theatre.

'When Benny started doing TV shows in the 'fifties and began to make a name for himself, he went out in variety on the Moss Empire circuit,' recalls comedian Max Bygraves. 'I went over to see him at Wood Green Empire, and I thought he was excellent.

'Benny has always pretended he hasn't got an act for the stage, but he was bloody marvellous. He could pack the place if he decided to give live shows, but he doesn't want to know about it.

'His heart has never been in the theatre or in the clubs. I think Benny would really have liked to make his career in films, but he took the next best thing. When he discovered the medium of television, he concentrated on that alone.'

Veteran funnyman Reg Varney, to whom Benny

acted as straight man on the music-halls, is convinced that his old partner found it an ordeal to face an audience on his own. 'He hated doing his own spot, hated doing stand-up comedy,' said Reg.

The perils of facing a live audience in provincial variety theatres, as Benny did in his early days, still bring shudders to performers like Bob Monkhouse.

'Being the opening comic could be like death,' says Monkhouse. 'There would be the overture, the speciality act — maybe a couple of girl dancers — and then suddenly you were out there on your own, struggling for laughs and not getting any.

'Maybe that's where Benny developed a certain shyness, a tendency to talk during the silences that might follow his punchlines. He had this private smile which said that he hadn't meant to get a laugh with that particular joke anyway, and you were an idiot if you did laugh at it.'

Monkhouse remembers visiting Benny backstage in a show called *Fine Fettle* at the Palace Theatre in London, and they stood in the wings watching singer Shani Wallis do her act. 'Look at her,' said Benny, enviously. 'She can't wait to go on, can't wait to get out there. Me, I can't wait to get OFF.'

Says Monkhouse: 'I have always felt that Benny never wanted to leave the quiet, dark confines of the wings to walk on the stage and into the spotlight and thrust what he had to offer at 2,000 people.

'One of Benny's difficulties was working in a big theatre. He needed to be intimate. That's one of the reasons the camera works for Benny.

'I remember that in that *Fine Fettle* show he did an

impersonation of Frankie Laine, the American singer, doing a song called 'Mule Train'. Benny said he loved doing the number because it allowed him to fling his arms around on stage. It was as though he had to take on the persona of a singer in order to feel uninhibited.

'It wasn't an audience he wanted to talk to. It was a camera. I believe Benny never focused on an audience in his life. I think Benny used to throw his eyes out of focus, and work to the back wall or into space.

'I don't think he ever wanted to see someone scowling, or sitting there with arms folded, or even someone laughing.

'He was waiting for that television camera to come along, and when it did all heaven broke loose.

Benny's refusal to do too much work has often puzzled agents and promoters who cannot understand why a comedian who can literally name his own price repeatedly turns down lucrative engagements.

But Benny is acutely aware of the dangers of over-exposure. He has never forgotten the advice given to him 30 years ago by impresario Lord Delfont: 'Don't make yourself too available. Do the important shows.'

Another show business encounter many years ago also helped to shape Benny's philosophy about the entertainment business. He was strolling in London's Regent's Park when a chauffeur-driven car carrying female impersonator Danny La Rue pulled up alongside him.

'Danny told me he was travelling to a matinee in Coventry, then he would be back to star in the West End, after which he had a show to give at his own night club,' Benny remembers.

'After he'd gone, I thought about it and decided I was better off looking at the trees and working at half steam.' Benny's approach has changed little since then, and he keeps work to a minimum. 'It might be different if I had a wife who kept saying she had nothing to wear, a chauffeur-driven Rolls-Royce and a bunch of kids at Eton,' he explains. 'But I have none of those expensive toys. I'm a bachelor, with no one to support.'

Back in the 1960s, Benny harboured an ambition to become a big star in continental comedy films, a dream inspired by seeing Jacques Tati in *Monsieur Hulot's Holiday*.

Benny explained: 'I'd like to walk past some Continental cinema showing a big picture of me outside and have people nudge each other as they see me in person and say: That's 'im, le great Benny Hill...'

The success of his television show in France has secured him such recognition in a somewhat different way, but that does not prevent him from viewing other French performers with a certain amount of envy. And the objects of his admiration might well indicate that, beneath the clown's exterior, there is a romantic soul struggling for release.

For Benny is a great fan of French singers Charles Aznavour and George Brassens. 'Even though they were not youngsters they were allowed to sing romantic songs,' he observes. 'Whereas if I got up and seriously began to sing "I Carry The Memory of You In My Heart Always", everyone would fall about laughing.'

It has been known for people to fall about laughing

at another aspect of Benny's life, and that is his penchant for never wasting anything, be it an unused gag or the remains of a tube of toothpaste. On the face of it there is a hint of madness or meanness about a millionaire who insists on returning home with a partially used bar of soap from the bathroom of a posh hotel.

Show business friends still tell the story of the day Benny asked agent Peter Charlesworth to give him a lift to the East End of London. They drove to a scruffy back street where a queue of people were waiting outside a shabby little shop. Benny was instantly recognised, and allowed to go to the front of the queue. He emerged minutes later, triumphantly clutching two sacks full of tinned food.

'The labels have come off the tins, you see,' explained Benny. 'So, because no one knows what's inside, they sell them off cheap.'

And so he drove back to his fashionable London flat, eager to open a tin or two to discover whether they contained baked beans or pineapple chunks.

While acknowledging that his family didn't have much cash to spare, Benny himself is baffled as to where he acquired such cautious and almost parsimonious habits. 'You'll never see any waste food in my house, not so much as a piece of stale bread or a bruised lettuce leaf,' he confesses. 'I'll eat anything rather than see it go to waste. I don't know why. It's not as if I had an underprivileged childhood or anything.'

Certainly the acquisition of half-used bars of soap and tins with no labels is not an indication of an avaricious nature. The man who could afford to have everything has in fact accumulated very little in the way of personal possessions.

The flat where he lived for more than 20 years in Queen's Gate, Kensington, retained a positively spartan look until *TV Times* magazine splashed out £5,000 to have it decorated for a 'Benny Hill at Home' feature.

'Benny has always lived in the sort of place where you feel you can take your boots off,' says script writer Dave Freeman. 'And that's Benny's best quality — he's always tolerant, easy going.'

Benny doesn't own a car, and his most treasured possession is the small diamond ring his father gave him on his 21st birthday. He never appears on TV without it.

'I don't like possessions cluttering up the place,' he says simply. 'People get funny about possessions. I once met a millionaire who was mean about toilet paper. If he thought anyone had gone to the loo in his house and used more than three sheets, he got annoyed. Can you imagine that?'

His antipathy towards motor cars also dates back to his Army service, when he was a driver-mechanic. 'I went over Europe's potholes for almost four years in every kind of vehicle,' he says.

'I drove everything from motorcycles and jeeps to dirty great six-wheelers, so I know a bit about driving. Once, in Germany, I gave a lift to a young French nurse and began showing off. We had a narrow escape, skidding off the road and then skidding back on. "Oh, monsieur, how pale you have gone," said the nurse. I was a reckless nit, so I became a full-time pedestrian.

'Anyway, if I bought a Rolls-Royce I would be for ever wondering if it was being scratched. I prefer to walk, or travel by bus or taxi.'

Benny studiously avoids discussion of his own personal wealth, suggesting: 'I don't think it's very nice talking about how much money you've got, do you?'

But the fact is that shrewd investment, plus the recurring royalties from a show which is seen in 90 countries have made him a multi-millionaire several times over. Some clue to his enormous earnings was provided in a conversation with a journalist friend after a newspaper published a list of the top ten TV earners in Britain in 1987. 'Jimmy Tarbuck was at the top of the list because he apparently earns a million pounds a year,' chuckled Benny.

'I wasn't even on the list. I was off it. Between you and me, I was off the top of it!'

To Benny's obvious discomfort, *Money Magazine*, in February, 1988, named him as one of the 200 wealthiest people in Britain, a list which was headed by the Queen (estimated wealth £3,286 million) and included *Dynasty* star Joan Collins (£15 million) and *Phantom of the Opera* composer Andrew Lloyd Webber (£25 million).

Benny's fortune was said to be £10 million, and he crept into the tail-end of the list alongside people like *Day of The Jackal* author Frederick Forsyth, actor Sean Connery of James Bond fame, actor Dudley Moore and former world champion racing driver Jackie Stewart.

'Benny Hill can out-earn anybody else on British

TV for the simple reason that you do not have to be British to understand him,' reported *Money Magazine*. 'His comedy show, made by Thames Television, has been sold to over 90 countries.

'In the UK his talent brought in gross revenues of £1.1 million in 1985. The 1986 figure was probably higher than that because, even after tax, his Benny Hill Entertainments company showed a profit of £933,073.'

For a man like Benny, who jealously guards his privacy, the publicity given to the *Money Magazine* list was annoying in the extreme.

'Filthy Rich' bellowed a headline two inches high on Page One of the *Sun*. Below was a picture of a bemused-looking Benny and the message: 'Saucy Benny is now a millionaire 10 times over.'

Reluctant to meet reporters eager to discuss the details of his financial affairs, Benny retreated behind the doors of the Thames Television studios in Teddington where he pronounced himself 'too busy' editing a new show to meet the Press.

But he did finally give one interview, and ironically it was to the newspaper which had branded him 'Filthy Rich'- the *Sun*.

'All this attention about my money has made a happy man very old,' Benny joked. 'But maybe I'll get a few proposals of marriage out of it — I reckon I must be the oldest eligible bachelor in town.

'I don't like talking about money, but everyone at the studio has been discussing little else. I am the most popular man around.

'They've been offering me boxes of chocolates and

chairs to sit on in the hope that they'll be mentioned in my will.

'My old mate Dennis Kirkland, the producer of the show, and I have had a running gag. He's been asking "Have you signed it yet then, Benny" and I keep telling him that it's all going to my co-star, little Jackie Wright.

'Seriously, I never knew what I was worth. I hope there are a few ladies out there prepared to make me an offer I can't refuse.'

Benny's protestations that he never really knew what he was worth had the ring of truth about them. For money certainly doesn't seem to mean much to the man who began his show business career earning £1 a night in working men's clubs. When a friend inquired how much he had lost in the Stock Market slump of 1987, he replied airily: 'I couldn't tell you.'

'He says that what he likes about having money is being able to choose to go wherever he wants,' says his neighbour, Mrs Moore. 'If he wants to pop over to Paris for a meal, he can do so. Or he can fly out to Australia, and not worry about the expense. He feels money has given him the choice of doing just what he likes.'

While not given to spectacular generosity, Benny is known for small, thoughtful gestures which seem to mean just as much to the recipients.

His Southampton neighbour, Mrs Moore, who helped him out with water supplies when the pipes froze at Christmas was delighted to find that when Benny returned a borrowed bucket it contained a bottle of vintage champagne.

After recruiting children belonging to members of his TV production team to act in some sketches, he went into a Southampton store and ordered toys to be sent to every one of the youngsters who had taken part.

For several years Benny's pint-sized TV stooge, Jackie Wright, was too ill to work on the programme. But viewers never noticed, because the little bald man who is for ever being smacked on the head by Benny still appeared in almost every show.

Benny insisted that previously unused film clips featuring Jackie should be slotted into the show. It meant that the diminutive performer would continue to be paid and, more importantly, it was a great boost to the ailing actor's morale to see himself on the screen.

In the days when he was struggling to make a name for himself as a comic, soon after the war, Benny happened to meet Harry Segal, the army sergeant who had given him his big break with the Forces show in Germany. Segal, also an aspiring entertainer, desperately needed £25 to buy some costumes which could clinch an important part for him in pantomime. Benny didn't hesitate to give him the cash, money with which he could ill afford to part.

'Absolute loyalty, that's what Benny has,' says his agent, Richard Stone. 'And he shows concern for others.'

The caring side of his character is something Benny Hill prefers to keep quiet about. He was mortified when a journalist discovered that for many years he had secretly been befriending two handicapped fans.

One of them was a disabled lady called Netta Warner, with whom he began corresponding after she sent him a Christmas card almost 30 years ago.

They had been corresponding for some years when Benny discovered that Netta, then aged 41, had never walked unaided. 'When he realised, he said he was coming to see her,' said her mother, Mrs Nell Warner. 'We never expected a big star like him to come, but he did.'

It was the first of many visits Benny made to the Warners' terraced house in South Wigston, Leicester. He would take Netta for walks in her wheelchair, sometimes stopping for lunch at one of the city's best restaurants.

The visits were made with the minimum of fuss, not to attract attention. It was only by chance that the secret slipped out, and when it did Benny was reluctant to discuss it.

'There is nothing worse than "Look at me, I'm dancing, look at me I'm doing good", is there?' he inquired.

Pressed for details, he added: 'Netta first wrote to me as a fan, and I started talking to her on the phone. She did not tell me that she was handicapped. When I found out and went to visit her I saw she was living in a little house with her parents and had to look at four walls most of the day because she could not get about.'

It emerged that, over the years, Benny had befriended four other women in similar circumstances. One of them was Phoebe King, from Felixstowe in Suffolk, who was also disabled and had to use a wheelchair.

She had met Benny when he was doing a summer show in Felixstowe in 1952, and Benny had come out of the theatre to meet her because she had difficulty getting to the stage door.

'Since then we have become great friends,' said Phoebe. 'He comes up whenever he can and pushes me for miles in my wheelchair, sometimes stopping off somewhere for a drink.'

Benny went to great lengths to make sure nothing stood in the way of his regular visits to Phoebe. He was due to travel up from Southampton to Felixstowe on the day the Duke and Duchess of York were married. Fearing the wedding traffic would prevent him getting across London to change trains, he hired a taxi to take him all the way to Felixstowe and back — a round trip of some 350 miles.

From time to time he brought Phoebe and Netta down to London, entertaining them at the Savoy Hotel. 'There are a lot of difficulties,' Benny confided to Fleet Street television writer Margaret Forwood.

'I have to do a recce first to find out which restaurants have no stairs and that sort of thing. Wheelchairs are heavy so I get into training before they come.

'But then I think that I have got these problems for a few days at a time. They have got to live with their handicaps all their lives.'

He added: 'It began out of a sense of duty. Now I enjoy their company. You've got to give back a little in this world, you can't just take all the time.'

Then, as an afterthought: 'Besides, it's nice taking ladies to dinner who don't complain about the food or burden you with their problems.'

Certainly there were no complaints from his neighbour in Southampton, 83-year-old Mrs Alice Moore, who has been an occasional guest of Benny's for lunch at the Wessex Hotel in Winchester.

'He took my sister and me there, and made us both feel like the Queen of England,' recalls Mrs Moore.

'I remember once the head waiter inquired whether we were related and Benny said: "Of course not, these are my Hill's Angels!" Oh, we couldn't stop laughing at that.'

If Benny displays similar consideration and concern for performers auditioning for his television show, it's because he vividly remembers similar ordeals he underwent himself in his early days in show business.

No matter how unpromising the newcomers might be, he always gives them a fair chance to show what they can do.

'I can appreciate what they are feeling,' he explains. 'Sometimes a producer would take an instant dislike to me. Before I could finish my stuff, he would snarl: "That's enough. Goodbye." So I don't have any of that.'

One thing Benny doesn't care for is the ostentatious lifestyle normally expected of the rich and the famous. While other stars might opt for the showy luxury of country mansions or Park Lane penthouses, the unassuming Mr Hill seems quite content to make his base the nondescript three bedroomed house in Southampton where he was brought up with his brother and sister.

When the lease on his flat in Kensington ran out in

1986, he didn't bother finding another swank address but headed straight for the old family home in Westrow Gardens. It is there, seated at the kitchen table, that he writes his scripts and deals with all his own correspondence.

Editors of America's *Time* magazine, who wrote from New York requesting an interview, were surprised to receive a handwritten reply from Benny scrawled on a piece of cheap lined paper which looked as though it had been torn from a school exercise book.

'This is a man who is essentially frugal,' suggests Bob Monkhouse. 'He arrives at rehearsals and gives people an orange or banana.

'It's the Getty effect, as if to say: "I am very rich and everyone expects me to spend a lot of money, so I won't".

'You know, he once told me that his idea of heaven was putting on a record of French concertina music, lighting up a Wills Whiff, opening a bottle of vin ordinaire and sitting there with his feet up on furniture which someone had given him free of charge for opening their shop.' Behind the neat lace curtains of Westrow Gardens, Benny Hill is alone with memories of both his mother and father, who died in the 1970s. He promised his mother he would never sell the house, and it's a vow he has kept.

Invitations from neighbours to join them in a drink at Christmas or at other holiday times are, in the main, politely refused. The man who amuses millions is happiest far away from the madding crowd.

'One New Year's Eve, instead of going to a party I

sat down with a bottle of wine and my diary to discover the nicest thing that had happened to me all year,' he told one interviewer.

'And do you know what was the most memorable thing? A tree which I had seen while out walking. Something about its shape, the way it was mottled in the sun.

'It was beautiful. A tree. The best thing in my life. Can you believe it?'

The house remains very much as it was when his mother died, with one of the downstairs rooms used as a bedroom just as it was in the days when it had to be converted for Mrs Hill because crippling arthritis prevented her climbing stairs.

For the last few years of her life, Benny's mother was in a nursing home. Benny visited her there regularly, taking her for walks in a wheelchair on Southampton Common.

Both Mr and Mrs Hill basked in the success of their son as he climbed to fame. The misgivings they had held when he set out for London with his little cardboard suitcase had long been forgotten.

Mr Hill had got into the habit of buttonholing local people, in the street or on a bus, and demanding: 'Did you see my son on TV last night?'

Those unwary enough to confess that they had in fact missed the *Benny Hill Show* were treated to a full enactment by the enthusiastic Mr Hill, complete with a full description of what Benny had been wearing and some graphic reconstructions of the faces he had pulled.

Similar action replays, with the personable shop

manager playing all the parts, were enacted among fellow members of the Banister and Old Green social clubs in Southampton.

Benny's father became his greatest fan. When Mr Hill, by then in his seventies, had to go into hospital, visitors noticed that a signed photograph of Benny was propped up on every bedside locker in the ward. Mr Hill had handed them out, to make sure his fellow patients were in no doubt about just whose son Benny Hill was.

The death of his mother was a bitter blow to Benny, and the circumstances were such that it could well have been that Mrs Hill sensed that the end was near.

The ailing old lady had specially asked Benny to take her out of the nursing home for a few days, because she wanted to see again the house in Westrow Gardens where she had brought up her family. She had only been inside the house a few hours when she died, with Benny by her side.

She was buried in Southampton cemetery, alongside her husband who had died some years earlier. Benny, head bowed, stood sad and silent between his elderly Aunt Louisa and Mrs Alice Moore.

'He was composed, but you could see that he was crying inside,' said Mrs Moore.

Throughout his climb to television stardom, Benny had stayed close to both his parents. He was delighted when he could afford to send them on a world cruise which included a stopover in Australia to visit their married daughter Diana, who had emigrated after working as a nurse at Southampton Eye Hospital. She later died of leukaemia.

A few years before his Dad died in 1971, Benny took him on a trip to Spain, and father and son stayed up until the wee small hours, seeking out the excitement of Madrid. They went to a night club, and when the cabaret finished at 2 am the somewhat disappointed 'Captain' asked: 'Isn't there any more?'

So they stayed on for the late show, and then Mr Hill insisted that they ignore the cruising taxis and instead walk back to their hotel through the deserted streets of the historic Spanish city.

Says Benny: 'I have this lovely picture in my mind of my old man, pushing 80, stepping out at dawn along the Gran Via.'

These days Benny sees very little of his brother Leonard, a retired schoolmaster. His closest relative is his Aunt Louisa, to whom he takes presents and flowers when he visits her home in Bexleyheath.

Benny has always been a loner. 'His isolation was always there,' suggests comedian Bob Monkhouse, who has known him for 30 years.

'I remember first meeting him soon after the war, and he was a very inhibited fellow, not too sure of his social graces. And in the 1940s if you hadn't had the kind of upbringing which taught you to use the correct fork at a dinner party or in a restaurant it could be a social embarrassment. People were snobbish about that sort of thing.

'Benny was always much more comfortable in a fish and chip joint or a salt beef restaurant than somewhere too posh, too grand.'

Benny seems never to have shed the shyness of those early days or the reluctance to allow outsiders into his life.

'You could always sense a discomfort when he was with other people,' says Monkhouse.

'If a relationship began to get deep, or expect more from him than he was ready to give in any way, he would back off very politely.

'He always eludes the grasp of people who want to make him into something he isn't, like a social animal or an eager-to-work show business celebrity. He has refused to dance to anybody else's tune.

'If he shows up at show business functions, he'll be the one at the back, quietly drinking a glass of water rather than wine.

'He is not at all gregarious, and he's never been a drinking man. On the few occasions he socialised with me I never thought he was particularly at ease. He once came to my home in St John's Wood in London and after a couple of drinks he became quite goofy quite rapidly and said his head was going round. He stepped outside for some fresh air and never came back.'

Nowadays, though, Benny is able to handle booze much better. 'On his birthday there's champagne all the way,' says producer Dennis Kirkland. 'It's "good morning, have a glass of champagne", and the rest of the day is a wipeout.'

Dennis recalls the day when a Belgian journalist came to the Thames studios to do an interview with Benny and brought a litre of vodka as a gift. Benny helped drink the bottle. 'But at the end of the day, everyone was legless except Benny,' said Dennis.

Despite his reluctance to become too involved socially, there is something intrinsically likeable about Benny Hill. 'He is someone you take to right away,' confirms Monkhouse. 'He has a quality about him which is tremendously attractive.

'I think anyone who has ever worked with him has a great deal of affection for him. But at the same time he keeps you at bay. There will be a glance, or an attitude or something which, even at his friendliest moments, distances you a little bit.'

Another of Benny's contemporaries, Max Bygraves, admits that he finds the Hampshire entertainer 'very deep', adding: 'On any show business occasion, like a Royal Command Performance or something, he always shuffles in very quietly.'

Meeting up with Max and others who shared his postwar struggle for recognition, Benny talks nostalgically and nonstop about the people and places their lives revolved around when they were show business newcomers eager for work. He has an amazing memory for detail, and can recall the name of every single person in the BBC contracts department of 30 years ago.

When he and his old music-hall partner, Reg Varney, happened to meet in Australia after they both became household names in Britain, it was not the rewards of stardom but the striving for success which Benny savoured most.

'The fun of getting there when you are young is great,' suggested Benny, fondly recalling even the ordeal of going out to face an audience when he was half sick with stage fright.

But such genial encounters are few and far between.

At the house in Southampton, the lights often burn until 2 am as Benny, a hermit-like figure, scribbles his scripts on scraps of paper or watches late night films on TV.

Occasionally he will emerge to pick up a takeaway meal from the nearby Kentucky Fried Chicken or walk down to Bedford Place to do his own shopping which he carries back home in a plastic bag.

'You would never think he was a multi-millionaire,' suggests Mrs Margaret Ball, another of his neighbours. 'He doesn't look like an international superstar. He looks as if he is on his uppers, like an old age pensioner who is just scraping by.'

Sometimes he takes a 15p bus ride into the city centre. But more often than not he walks, alone and unrecognised with dark glasses disguising the familiar chubby face. He regularly visits Southampton cemetery, tenderly laying fresh flowers on the grave where his mother and father lie buried side by side.

On a fine day you are likely to find him striding through the New Forest, content with his own company. His favourite place is St Catherine's Hill, a peaceful, scenic spot overlooking the cathedral city of Winchester.

'He walks miles, not because he is mean but because he is conscious of putting on weight,' explains his producer, Dennis Kirkland.

'He might walk a few miles and then pop into a shop for some newspapers and a couple of Mars bars.'

Says Benny: 'When I go out for the Sunday papers, I take the longest route possible. When I reckon I've walked off the equivalent of a Mars bar — around 295 calories — I buy one and eat it.

'My love of sweet things started when I was a teenager. I used to go to the cinema twice a week and buy six cakes for fourpence. Then I'd have a choc-ice and a milk chocolate bar. These days I'll have a bran bar for breakfast — only 12 calories. Then, if I have a salad lunch, I'll go for low calorie cottage cheese and pineapple.'

Benny has worried about his weight ever since he overheard two showgirls talking about him more than 30 years ago when he was doing a summer season at Great Yarmouth. 'That Benny Hill is nice,' observed one of the dancers. 'But isn't he fat?'

But at the age of 64 he has almost given up fighting the flab. When he went to visit his old friend Mrs Lillywhite in Southampton, she remarked: 'My word, you HAVE got tubby.'

'That's very kind of you, but you needn't wrap it up,' shrugged Benny. 'I'm just fat.'

Weight problems apart, the cheerful comedian has always enjoyed good health, apart from an operation on a troublesome kidney and a spell in hospital in 1983 with internal bleeding from a stomach ulcer.

As Benny Hill buries himself more and more in his work, outward appearances seem to matter less and less. He realises that the Benny Hill who people really care about is the saucy, outrageous and mischievous character they see on their TV screens.

'I remember I once wrote an article about the two great love affairs in my life that went wrong,' he recalls. 'A woman wrote to me from Bradford, saying: "We don't want to know about your bloody broken heart."

She was right. My job is to be interesting, funny and throw in a pinch of social comment — in that order.'

If Benny Hill is still nursing a broken heart, he certainly doesn't want the fact paraded in public or to be suddenly confronted with reminders of the past while the whole world watches. Attempts have twice been made to feature him as the subject of *This Is Your Life* on television, but on each occasion Benny found out about it and blocked the project.

'I should just be so bloody embarrassed,' he told Fleet Street television writer Geoff Baker.

'I would cry the very second anyone came on. You just don't know who is going to turn up. They would dig up anyone I've been half nice to, on would come the wheelchairs and there wouldn't be a dry seat in the place.

'I don't want to put myself through that — and they don't pay you to do it, either.'

One puzzling point encountered by the researchers for *This Is Your Life* was Benny's exact age. His biography issued by Thames Television gives his date of birth as January, 1925, and most reference books also list that date. In fact he was born exactly a year earlier, in January 1924.

If this is a deliberate deception, it seems an out-of-character quirk for someone who cares little for outward appearances and who feels no need to maintain any kind of off-screen image.

Disappointing the public is the thing which bothers him most, and it is this determination and desire to please which fuels his incessant search for professional perfection.

'The television audience has become terribly choosy,' he points out. 'Without moving out of their chairs, without forking out a halfpenny except for their licence fee — they see the greatest artistes in the world.

'And remember, one poor sketch and the criticism crashes around your ears like granny's brolly. For there is no real glamour about TV, none of the intangible, romantic remoteness which surrounds a film star.

'You're too close to the public in that little box. They've got you at their mercy with a switch.

'If 11 million people have seen you in their parlours, the chances are you're bound to run into some of them next day. And they tell you dead straight what they think of you, as if they own you, as if they'd been personal friends for years.'

While others may seek to analyse the enigma of Benny Hill, his fellow professionals are content to assess him purely on the performances which have made him an astounding international success.

'He's the best television comic or comic performer we've got,' insists his producer, Dennis Kirkland. 'He may not be the funniest man or the best entertainer. But he's definitely the best performer. Mime, songs, poetry, sketches, stand-up comedy — you name it, he does it.'

Ken Seddington, who has worked as his stand-in on his TV show, suggests: 'Benny is a genius. He's funny all the time, whether he's on screen or not. I can never remember him, in 15 years, being morose.

'He loves to perform, whether it's to a TV audience of 10 million, a lunchtime audience of half a dozen —

or just one.'

Impresario Lord Delfont declares: 'You can't analyse it. I first saw Benny many years ago in Margate, when he was a straight man to Reg Varney. I just knew then that he had a unique quality.'

Reg Varney remembers those days, too. 'Even then, Benny was a loner, a person to himself,' he says. 'But as a performer, he was so clever, with the ability to adapt material and give it a personal twist.

'I wasn't surprised he became so big. I can remember even now thinking that there was a kind of magic there somewhere. He had this great talent for writing and he was outstanding doing bits of comedy "business". It was a great combination, and I knew he was really going to make something of himself.'

It's the sheer inventiveness of the man which Bob Monkhouse admires most. 'I think a great deal of what he does is intuitive,' he explains. 'But then layer on layer is added to that as he discovers new ways to get laughs, new ways to be effective.

Script writer Dave Freeman, who worked on the early Benny Hill shows, is in no doubt about the enduring magic of the man who has put a smile on the face of the entire world.

'Benny is a born performer,' he says. 'If he doesn't do too much of it, he could last on TV for ever.'

There seems little danger of Benny doing too much TV, even though America is crying out for more material to feed the 80 stations who are still showing his old shows over and over again. Three hour-long shows a year for Thames is about all he plans to do.

'I've no ambitions to become the richest man in the

cemetery,' insists Benny. 'If I worked any harder, then I'd just be knocking myself out for the taxman.'

Growing old alone holds no fears for the man with hardly any family and very few friends.

'My sister was always saying that because I wasn't married there would be no one to cry at my funeral,' he says. 'That suits me fine. I don't want anyone to cry at my funeral.'

CHAPTER
TEN

Around the World

Benny Hill sat alone outside a back street café in Marseilles, sipping a glass of wine and scribbling an idea for a sketch on the back of a dog-eared menu.

Out of the corner of his eye, he sensed a slight movement in the scruffy street and this was accompanied by the sound of half-stifled giggling. Moments later a line of laughing street urchins came parading by his table, walking jerkily as if in a silent film and delivering Fred Scuttle salutes.

'Benneee Heeeel!' screeched the members of this maniacal march-past, collapsing in even more giggles as Benny recognised them with a friendly wave and they disappeared, strutting and laughing and screwing their faces up into lustful leers in a perfect parody of the ending to a Benny Hill television show.

Such encounters have become commonplace for Benny Hill, whose television shows are seen in more than 80 countries.

In France, even the attractions of l'amour have been known to take second place to the lure of Benny Hill, and many a mistress who assumed that her partner's impatience to whisk her back to her apartment early in the evening stemmed from unbridled passion has been dismayed to discover that the real reason for such unseemly haste was that he didn't want to miss the *Benny Hill Show* on Channel Three.

When Benny is spotted on holiday in St Tropez, even the fashionable yacht-owning sophisticates of the French Riviera queue for his autograph.

His early appearances on French television in 1980 were considered somewhat indelicate even by the standards of Frenchmen whose attitude to sexual matters has always been considered liberal. One critic labelled him 'the king of vulgarity' and another said he had 'the finesse of a bulldozer'.

But, as so often happens, the public ignored the carping of the critics and warmed to the antics of the moon-faced British clown whose intentions needed no translation.

Playing opposite major news programmes on the two rival Paris channels on a Sunday night, Benny retains a faithful following in France, where the programme is dubbed into French. 'No, I don't think the French find him shocking,' says Madame Bettina Olivier, of Channel Three. 'But he is funny, maybe a little saucy. And, of course, French men like to see lots of girls with nice legs.'

Big business wasn't slow to catch on to the commercial potential of the funny little Englishman with the expressive eyebrows. Sales of Jacques Brunch biscuits in France soared after the company paid Benny £80,000 to appear in ten 30-second commercials on TV. 'He has an amazing quality of changing his appearance,' enthused Pierre Berge, head of the agency which made them.

Benny also has a huge following in Greece, where his ratings matched those of *Dallas*. He was inundated with fan mail when a leading Greek television magazine featured him on their cover and encouraged their readers to write to him by printing a suitable sample letter in English.

Sales of German Kaiser beer trebled in Greece when the brewery discarded three leading actors who had been starring in their TV commercials and replaced them with Benny, who received £25,000 for one and a half days' filming.

Athens police had to move in to control a huge crowd when a TV crew making a commercial for video cassettes started filming him among the ruins of the Acropolis. Benny was dressed as a member of the Tsolias, the kilted presidential guards who wear shoes tipped with pompoms.

Enraged by the idea of a revered national monument being used as the background for a TV commercial, it looked as though the police were about to arrest the entire crew. But the incident ended in laughter when the officers spotted Benny, crowded round for his autograph, and then found them a more suitable spot for filming on a nearby hillside.

Spaniards are equally enthusiastic about Señor Hill. The success of his show there was followed by a series of commercials for a Spanish-made TV set in which

Benny played British, German, Italian and Japanese characters, all despondently discovering that, when it comes to making TVs, Spanish is best.

Australians love Benny Hill, and they were one of the first overseas countries to buy the programme from Britain. A chain of stores called Waltons, who sell everything from lingerie to hardware, signed him up for a hugely successful series of commercials in which he appeared as a lion tamer, a trapeze artist, a cleaning lady and a schoolboy.

Almost every corner of the globe has at one time or another been exposed to the *Benny Hill Show*. Among the countries who have bought it from Thames Television are Brunei, Chile, Israel, Hong Kong, Hungary, Nicaragua, Poland, and Venezuela. Some Russians also manage to tune in by pointing their aerials towards Finland.

Such exposure has made Benny the best-known comedian in the world, outstripping Charlie Chaplin and other legendary figures who did not have the advantage of modern communications.

'It is literally true that there are big American cities where it is possible to watch the *Benny Hill Show* every night,' reported Simon Hoggart in *New Society* magazine in January, 1985. 'Last year I switched on the TV in our hotel room in Peking, and there it was again, piped from goodness knows where, filling in the gap between two films.'

Benny Hill was sold to China's Guandong Television after Thames Television screened the show for delegates at the Third World Advertising Congress in Peking. 'Benny Hill had the Chinese delegates standing five deep around the stand, roaring with laughter,' said Peter Davies, sales director of Thames Television International.

Similar laughter engulfed a Russian delegation at the Montreux TV festival in 1984, but with less fortunate results. A member of the Soviet State Committee for radio and television appeared to anger fellow delegates by laughing too long and too loud at Benny's jokes.

Staff at the hotel were amazed by what happened next. 'It was frightening,' said receptionist Patricia Fierro. 'A large, military looking man demanded to see our Russian guest. He took him outside and they had an argument. Then he was pushed into a car and driven off.'

When last seen, the hapless Russian was being escorted to a Moscow-bound plane by a large gentleman in a dark KGB style overcoat.

Everything — even war — seems to stop for Benny Hill. Bob Saget of CBS television in New York says: 'One of our news people based in Beirut told us that when Benny Hill comes on Syrian television, every antenna in the Middle East turns towards Damascus, and there is a *de facto* ceasefire along the Green Line. Having Benny Hill on 24 hours a day might keep the world laughing instead of fighting.'

In Iran, the Ayatollah Khomeini has officially made it a crime to watch Benny Hill, and an Iranian caught trying to smuggle Benny Hill tapes into the country was jailed.

Ironically, Benny Hill was one of the most popular figures on Argentinian television when Britain went to war with Argentina over the issue of the Falkland Islands in 1982. As the British task force sailed for the South Atlantic to recapture the islands from Argentinian occupation, viewers in Buenos Aires and elsewhere in the South American nation were chuckling over the antics of Benny and the gang.

'We were rehearsing in London when someone came in with an Argentinian TV magazine, and the girls and I were on the cover,' recounts Benny.

'It just goes to show how stupid war is when people can watch an English programme and have a good laugh and then, when it's all over, carry on with the business of killing each other.'

At the Montreux TV Festival in 1955, Benny was given a special award for the programme which has been sold to so many countries around the world.

With characteristic shyness, he made a brief speech, but did not linger long. A trip up a Swiss mountainside in a little cog-wheel train had given him an idea for a sketch with overtones of *The Sound of Music*, and he was anxious to get back to London to try it out.

If it worked, the chuckles would be heard from Croydon to Cuba.

CHAPTER
ELEVEN
King Leer

Veteran film producer Hal Roach didn't hesitate when he was asked to name a present-day performer who could be compared with comedy giants of yesteryear like Laurel and Hardy.

'I guess there's only one — Benny Hill,' he said. Then he added: 'But I wish he'd clean up his act.'

Trying to get Benny Hill to clean up his act has become a preoccupation for outraged moral crusaders, offended feminists, concerned parents and sundry other groups who have voiced their various objections to the antics of the comedian they call King Leer.

From Manchester to Miami, the *Benny Hill Show* has been accused of dabbling in vulgarity, lewdness, suggestiveness and downright dirt.

Nancy Banks-Smith of the *Guardian* zeroed in on one of Benny's programmes in 1972 and concluded: 'It is absolutely filthy.'

Such criticisms emanate from Mr Hill's ability to

introduce a smirk into almost every sketch. Facing the cameras as Amos Thripp, head gardener at Landerley Hall and a leading authority on the vegetable marrow, he announces slyly: 'I do hope, before the evening is over, to show the viewers my three foot, six inch wonder.'

Yes, he admits, grinning inanely from beneath the upturned brim of his battered hat, he had once been the proud possessor of a specimen which was four foot six inches long, 'but I was younger then. I wasn't married, and I had more time.'

Meanwhile, perhaps the viewers would like to see the new rose which he has grown. He calls it the Raquel Welch.

Is it nice in a bed?

'Well, it's quite nice in a bed,' concedes Benny, mouth twitching at the corners. 'But some people prefer it up against the wall.'

And so Amos Thripp leaves us with a final, stern warning: 'Just because winter draws on, that's no reason to discard your summer bloomers entirely.

'If Jack Frost gets his hands on your geraniums, by golly you'll know all about it.'

It is double-edged dialogue like that which has made Benny Hill the target of many a prurient complaint, but he remains unrepentant.

'My shows are good, robust comedy of the old music-hall kind,' he insists. 'I'm a down-to-earth comedian. Vulgar, perhaps, but certainly not obscene.

'I'm not a dirty old man. I hear or see things on other shows that I would never do.

'People make up their own jokes. I always include

a piece of graffiti on the wall behind me in my shows. One reads: "It's 12 inches long, but I don't use it as a rule." Some viewers complained, and almost everybody had mistaken what they thought they had read.

'I'm not a blue comic, I'm a saucy one.'

Too saucy for some. The Festival of Light, a moral reform group, complained to the Independent Television Authority about one of Benny's programmes. 'Mr Hill was shown in fancy dress in a sketch called "The Night Before And The Morning After",' sniffed Festival official Peter Thompson. 'On the morning after, he shoots his wife and then gets hold of a man and says "Come on, darling", or something like that.

'We felt there were rather degrading moral overtones to this. As a satire or comedy, we found it unjustified.'

Suggestions that he is a corrupter of public morals are deeply resented by Benny who sees things in a much more simplistic manner. 'You'll never see anything offensive or dirty in my shows, and you'll never hear any bad language,' he told television journalist Clifford Davis. 'I don't swear, and I don't use four-letter words. It's all suggestion.'

Nevertheless, even a country like Sweden, normally considered quite liberal when it comes to sexual matters, has been offended by the content of some of the shows. In 1986 some Swedes attacked the show for being pornographic, and demanded that it should be removed from peak viewing hours or even banned altogether.

'We have had a lot of complaints,' said a spokesman for Sweden's state-run TV channel.

Many feminists see the show as an endless exercise in the degradation of women, and in 1986 a survey by *Woman's Own* magazine named the Benny Hill programme as the one they disliked most — even more than sport on TV. 'Of all the results in the survey, Benny's unpopularity shocked us most,' said the magazine. 'The *Benny Hill Show* is a man's programme, and women could find it sexist. Many obviously do.'

Benny Hill's producer, Dennis Kirkland, dismissed the survey as of little consequence. 'If they think Benny's programme is sexist, then how about *Woman's Own* for a title,' he responded. 'Benny is loved all over the world, and it's not an anti-woman programme.'

Women, however, remained unconvinced. At a Trades Union Congress conference in Brighton, women delegates named Benny as the biggest male chauvinist on television. 'The show is all knickers and knockers,' wailed one.

Television clean-up campaigner Mrs Mary Whitehouse thought one programme in particular, in 1981, went too far and claimed: 'The dress, or lack of it, could be fairly described as soft porn. The dance sequences were of a kind associated with so-called adult night clubs, certainly not with family viewing.'

The Independent Broadcasting Authority replied: 'If we thought the *Benny Hill Show* was leading the way to pornography, then we would not allow the programme to be broadcast.

'We think it represents a very old tradition of broad humour which is particularly British but which some of our viewers find not to their taste.'

It is the Hill's Angels, with their raunchy dance routines, who seem to offend feminists most. They were introduced after the show took a change of direction in the mid '70s and Benny deliberately decided to introduce more glamour to the programme.

'For years I thought sexy girls would put off the women viewers,' he revealed. 'I stuck to pleasant girls like Anne Shelton and Petula Clark. Then I realised I wasn't doing the sort of show I would want to watch. So in came the girls.'

In fact the new policy was inspired by some on-screen comments from television announcer David Hamilton who introduced the *Benny Hill Show* with a note of envy in his voice.

'Lucky old Benny, surrounded by all those lovely ladies,' he said. The comment made Benny think that if David Hamilton was so taken with the girls, other viewers might feel the same way, and so he added more of them and began to include them in sketches.

'I like pretty girls in my shows,' he admits. 'I'm a seller of dreams. We're all in the business of dreams. Girls in dreams don't have pimples or bad breath.'

The idea that the sight of a lustful Benny chasing a scantily clad girl across a field poses some sinister threat to the status of women annoys him greatly.

'There is nothing nasty or sexist about my comedy,' he explained to Clifford Davis.

'And the fact that I chase the girls doesn't make me a dirty old man. The whole idea is based on the premise that I fail in my pursuit. Terrible things happen to me, apart from the disappointment of being rebuffed and not getting anywhere with my advances.

'This same frustration and failure happens to the other men in the show, like Bob Todd and Jackie Wright. We get doused with water from a hose, we fall down ladders, we fall in lakes, we fall off bicycles.

'I don't downgrade women. Quite the opposite. They downgrade me. On my shows it is always the men who suffer, never the girls. The girls score off us every time. We're always the losers.'

Similar sentiments were expressed by Benny when he discussed with Anthony Slide of *Gallery* magazine the constant criticism that his shows are sexist. 'It comes from people who haven't really looked at the show,' he insisted. 'Basically, it's the old men chasing the young girls — they never catch 'em. And it's the old men who are the fools.

'I mean, if I were to treat any of the girls the way I treat the men, there would be an outcry. Take the little fellow, Jackie Wright. I keep hitting him on the head, kicking him up the bum, banging him with lumps of wood. If I did that to a 20-year-old girl, it would be terrible, wouldn't it. It's not degrading for the women as much as the men.'

Benny was not alone in his defence of the show. Television critic James Wolcott in the New York *Village Voice* asserted: 'Except for a few coarse rape jokes, Benny Hill is free of female-loathing malice, and the women on his show seem to have ripping fun. Benny remembers that life's a nasty, treacherous comedy and sex a glorious joke.'

Kay Gardella of the New York *Daily News*, who confesses to being occasionally startled by the programme, cornered Benny for an interview while she was visiting London and reported: 'Some of the more straight-laced say his show is vulgar, shocking, sexist and maybe even a threat to the establishment. Hill blandly shrugs off such criticism. "I can't please everybody," he says. "I do the kind of show I like to watch myself. I compare the show to a box of chocolates. It's an assortment. You like some bits, you don't like others. But you don't throw the box away.

'"As for what might be objectionable, that's more a matter of geography than anything else. You wouldn't believe what you'll see and hear in a West German cabaret, but it's perfectly acceptable there.

'"The States are probably a little less tolerant than England, but I once counted 72 obscenities in one of your movies. Killing bulls is an art in Spain, a crime in England. So it goes.

'"I aim to have something for everyone. So if the gags aren't funny you can look at the girls. And if you don't think the girls are pretty, you can listen to the music."'

Look closely and you might even glimpse the occasional social comment among the stockings and suspenders. Benny was quite proud of a sketch about the National Health Service. 'We showed the National Health patients being herded into a slum building and bossed around, while the private patients had beautiful sexy nurses in saucy underwear pouring champagne for them,' he explained. 'Of course it was an exaggeration, but I think it was fair comment on the stark contrast between private medicine and the Health Service.'

While feminists raged against what they saw as the excesses of the *Benny Hill Show*, American television critics — the male ones, anyway — continued to chuckle fondly at the entertainer they dubbed the Bawdy Brit. Marvin Kitman of *Newsday* displayed withdrawal symptoms when the programme was temporarily unavailable in the New York area.

'He was the man who showed us how to do tasteless humour tastefully,' mused Mr Kitman. 'He used to make the night by patting his poor old geriatric sidekick on the head and patting the women everywhere.

'I love that gleam in his eye as he coped with all those girls in their scanties. He was so evil, malevolent and funny. Benny Hill's humour wasn't for the Bible belt. It was garter belt TV.'

Amid all the fuss and discussion over whether his shows are an unacceptable mixture of sexism and soft porn, Benny himself remains convinced that they are no more harmful than the saucy variety shows his grandad took him to when he was a schoolboy in Southampton.

'I can't understand people who make such accusations,' he protests. 'But I do know from letters that Thames Television and I receive that they are in a tiny minority.

'I think my shows are the last direct descendants of those saucy revues of the 1930s which also featured a comedian surrounded by beautiful girls. I remember them as a child. Not even the prudes of those days called them obscene.

'I have always thought of myself as a people's comic, not an intellectual one.'

And for the final proof that there is at least one woman who finds his show totally acceptable, Benny cites the example of the lady who sent him a book of poems, penned in praise of the programme.

It was dedicated to 'hit skits, tits and wits'.

CHAPTER
TWELVE

Yankee Doodle Dandy

'Hey, Benny, this way! Yeah, the silly grin, that's the one. Give us the grin again!'

Excitedly shouting instructions and jostling for position, the newspaper cameramen crowded onto the viewing platform at the top of the Empire State Building in Manhattan as Benny Hill posed for pictures wearing an inane Fred Scuttle smile and a T-shirt emblazoned with 'I Love New York'.

If confirmation were needed of Benny Hill's status as one of America's favourite adopted sons, it was provided by the hysteria which surrounded the shy British comedian on that sunny March morning in 1987. 'The Empire State building seemed in danger of toppling over as hordes of sightseers who had been gawping at the view suddenly spotted Benny and rushed over to gawp at him,' reported Margaret Forwood, TV writer of *The People* newspaper.

Benny faced the fuss with the patient and stoic

demeanour of a man who had seen it all before. Similar scenes had greeted his first-ever visit to the United States three years previously.

Beset by the persistent blandishments of Las Vegas hotel managements including the message from the Mafia man — Benny had strenuously resisted all attempts to lure him to America, even though the correspondence columns of American newspapers frequently carried plaintive letters from fans demanding to know when they could expect to see him in person.

However, curiosity finally overcame him, and in September 1984, he flew to New York on a three-week holiday with his producer, Dennis Kirkland. It was supposed to be purely a private visit, but America had other ideas. Despite his attempts to shelter anonymously behind a large pair of tinted spectacles, Benny was given a hero's welcome from the moment his plane touched down at Kennedy Airport.

'Hey, howdya like that, it's Benny Hill!' The cry from the customs man sent people racing across the airport concourse, straining for a glimpse of the British comic whose face was familiar from a hundred reruns of his television shows.

Adulation was everywhere. When he went to dinner at the swank Rainbow Room in Manhattan, the orchestra struck up the jaunty little tune which forms the background for the speeded-up sequence which traditionally ends a *Benny Hill Show*. A blue-rinsed matron gushed up to his table and insisted that she simply HAD to run her fingers through his hair.

While Benny may not have given tuppence for the chance to appear on Broadway, he soon fell under the spell of the Great White Way and embarked on a hectic round of show-going. The hit musical *My One and Only* was one of his first calls, and after the show he went out to dinner with its English star, Twiggy ('she paid — I love that in a woman', he mischievously told a television interviewer later).

Also on Benny's list was the nude revue *Oh, Calcutta!* 'What impressed me about him was the fact that although he was on holiday he never really stopped working,' recalls agent Don Taffner. 'Whether he was out catching a couple of shows or just sitting in my house watching television, he was always on the lookout for new ideas.

'He had this idea for a type of Gilbert and Sullivan sketch, and when he heard there was a Gilbert and Sullivan company from Canada in town he insisted on going to see their show.'

From New York, Benny and Dennis Kirkland flew to California, a trip which was to strike a somewhat disappointed note when Benny discussed it later with journalist Margaret Forwood in London. 'In three weeks in America I never met one pretty girl,' sighed Benny. 'There were just fellas everywhere. Each time we were invited out to a meal or party I said: "Will there be any girls?" But there never were.

'Would you believe, one night we went to a party at Hugh Hefner's, the *Playboy* boss, and still nothing happened. He came in and talked to us in his black pyjamas. Then he went off to bed and said: "Stay and enjoy yourselves." But the atmosphere was very virginal and innocent.

'One night we were invited out by Burt Reynolds

and some other chaps. I thought, this is bound to be all right. I mean, Burt Reynolds, after all.

'Would you believe it, the six of us fellas had dinner alone.'

Benny sounded equally frustrated when he spoke to Tim Ewbank of the *Sun*. 'Wherever we went there were never any girls,' moaned Benny. 'In Los Angeles I stayed at a hotel with a fabulous swimming pool. It was surrounded by sunbeds, and I thought that the next day they just had to be full with lovely girls.

'So I got up early and sat by the pool until three in the afternoon. You know what happened? The only person I saw was Bruce Forsyth!'

A slightly spicier version of Benny's Californian visit was provided by British journalist Terry Willows, who met up with Benny in San Francisco.

'Benny had hoped to slip quietly into the city and spend a quiet, relaxing holiday,' reported Willows. 'But what he didn't realise was that the *Benny Hill Show* was being shown on two different local TV stations every night.

'The locals loved him. Everywhere they called and waved to him, asked for his autograph and had him posing for snaps with babies and fat ladies.'

And though, on his return to London. Benny couldn't recall meeting any good-looking ladies on his American trip, he had clearly forgotten a stunning blonde-haired model called Laurie Tollefson.

Writing in the *Star* newspaper in London, Willows described how Benny and 23-year-old Laurie had walked hand in hand to lunch at a Mexican restaurant where Benny produced an impromptu serenade for his newfound friend. 'With a guitar in hand and red blanket over his shoulder, he plucked a few poignant chords and crooned sweet nothings in Laurie's ear,' reported Willows. 'Then, after a sharp shot of tequila, Benny took Laurie's hand and headed off for the Golden Gate bridge by taxi.'

It was certainly an unforgettable encounter for the lovely Laurie. 'When we first met, I couldn't stop laughing,' she said. 'He was the Benny Hill I watch twice every night on television.

'But as we walked the streets hand in hand, cuddled over lunch and spent a romantic day and evening I saw the real Benny Hill. He's a very loving and affectionate man.'

Despite the professed lack of ladies, Benny's meeting with actor Burt Reynolds had obviously been a big success. Reynolds, an avid Benny Hill fan, invited him to his Beverly Hills mansion and the two sat around drinking and swapping jokes.

Reynolds offered to appear on Benny's show and Benny forecast: 'If working with him is as funny as drinking with him, it will be hilarious.'

It was more than two years before Benny made another trip to America, and this time there was no hope at all of hiding behind dark glasses. The occasion, in March 1987, was a salute to Thames Television by the International Council of America's National Academy of Television Arts and Sciences in New York.

Benny overcame his reluctance to appear live on stage and agreed to take part in a show at the Lincoln Center in New York, alongside other British stars like impressionists Mike Yarwood and Janet Brown and actor Edward Woodward, star of *The Equalizer* TV series. Six Hill's Angels were also in the lineup, dressed in 'Pearly Queen' costumes.

The project got off to a singularly inauspicious start when mechanical problems caused a six-hour delay at Gatwick airport and Benny and the rest of the Thames party eventually had to board a bus and transfer to London's Heathrow Airport. But touchdown at New York's Kennedy airport sparked off an immediate bout of Benny Hill mania.

'Benny was mobbed, there's no other word for it,' recounted Margaret Forwood of the *People*, who travelled with the Thames party.

'A jumbo-load of tired and puzzled passengers stood in lengthening queues as immigration and customs officials left their posts to crowd around their chubby hero.'

Anxious to ensure that the gala stage show was a success, Benny headed straight for a rehearsal room in downtown Manhattan where he and the Hill's Angels ran through their routines. Benny could hardly remember his last live stage appearance, and he was understandably apprehensive about facing the Lincoln Center audience.

Constant requests for television interviews provided an unwanted distraction and when Bob Saget of the CBS Morning Programme did finally corner him in the rehearsal rooms for a brief chat, Benny appeared slightly uncomfortable and decidedly wary in front of the camera.

'Go on, ask me why I never got married,' urged

Benny, as if anxious to dispose of the question which every interviewer asked sooner or later.

'Okay,' said Saget. 'Why did you never get married?' A familiar sly grin began to creep across Benny's rotund face and he stared straight into the camera. 'Because I fly a lot, and I like a window seat,' he said.

Bob Saget was still trying to work that one out when the interview ended.

Benny's anxieties about the Lincoln Center stage show were unfounded. From the moment the audience caught the first glimpse of his impish smile they welcomed him like a national hero.

Marvin Kitman, television critic for *Newsday* and a long-time admirer of Benny Hill, reported: 'I was surprised he wasn't wearing a raincoat, and the black socks and garters or some other suitable attire from his TV repertoire. I guess he thought the high-echelon audience at Alice Tully Hall might be offended.

'He played a stage hand in an "I Love New York" T-shirt who kept interrupting a fellow in a tuxedo who was telling us how great Thames TV was. Also, he read to us from his diary about his experiences in New York. Very funny stuff.'

The newspapers wanted pictures of Benny against a New York background so, still wearing his I Love New York shirt, he travelled to the top of the Empire State building. Some 1,200 ft above the streets of Manhattan, Benny Hill leered into the clicking cameras, with a jumbo-sized pretzel in his hand and a French-style beret perched awkwardly on his head.

Eager fans reached out to touch him, and some of them were carrying copies of that morning's New

York *Daily News* in which TV critic Kay Gardella described Benny as 'one of the last practitioners of the ancient art of burlesque'.

Surrounded by this gawping crowd, Benny glanced up at the Empire State building's massive television mast spiking into the clear blue sky. There were thousands of masts like that all over America, beaming out the *Benny Hill Show* and putting a smile on the face of an entire nation.

It was hard to believe that it had all begun more than 50 years earlier when a lad called Alfred Hawthorn Hill sat entranced in the darkness of an English music-hall.

Savouring the moment, Benny Hill allowed himself a secret little smile of his own as he gazed into the distance from the dizzying height of the Empire State.

The schoolboy who dreamed of stardom was on top of the world.

Index

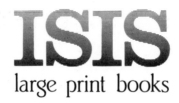

large print books

We hope that you have enjoyed this book and will want to read more.

We list some other titles on the next few pages. All our books may be purchased from ISIS at either of the addresses below.

If you are not already a customer, or on our mailing list, please write and ask to be put on the mailing list for regular information about new ISIS titles.

We would also be pleased to receive your suggestions for titles that you would like us to publish in large print. We will look into any suggestions that you send to us.

Happy reading.

ISIS, 55 St Thomas' Street, Oxford OX1 1JG, ENGLAND, tel (0865) 250333

BIOGRAPHY AND AUTOBIOGRAPHY

Bill Adler	**Fred Astaire**
Charles Allen	**Plain Tales from the Raj**
Chuck Ashman & Pamela Trescott	**Cary Grant**
Hilary Bailey	**Vera Brittain**
Trevor Barnes	**Terry Waite**
Winifred Beechey	**The Rich Mrs Robinson**
Cilla Black	**Step Inside**
Sydney Biddle Barrows	**Mayflower Madam**
Peter Harry Brown	**Such Devoted Sisters: Those Fabulous Gabors**
Patrick Campbell	**Selections from 35 Years on the Job**
Joe Collins	**A Touch of Collins**
Bill Cosby	**Time Flies**
George Courtauld	**Odd Noises from the Barn**
Mary Craig	**The Crystal Spirit: Lech Walesa and his Poland**
Peter Cushing	**An Autobiography**
Peter Cushing	**'Past Forgetting'**
Roald Dahl	**Going Solo**
Betty Davis	**This 'n' That**

BIOGRAPHY AND AUTOBIOGRAPHY

Peter Evans	**Ari: The Life and Times of Aristotle Socrates Onassis**
Diana Farr	**Five at 10: Prime Ministers' Consorts Since 1957**
David Fingleton	**Kiri**
Angela Fox	**Slightly Foxed**
Michael Freeland	**A Salute to Irving Berlin**
Joyce Fussey	**Cats in the Coffee**
Joyce Fussey	**'Milk My Ewes and Weep'**
Eve Garnett	**First Affections**
Jon Godden & Rumer Godden	**Two under the Indian Sun**
Unity Hall	**Philip**
Helen Hayes	**Loving Life**
Bob Hope	**Confessions of a Hooker**
Graham Jenkins	**Richard Burton, My Brother**
Penny Junor	**Charles**
Roger Kahn	**Joe and Marilyn**
Vincent V Loomis	**Amelia Earhart**
Suzanne Lowry	**Cult of Diana**
Ralph G Martin	**Charles & Diana**
John McCabe	**Mr Laurel and Mr Hardy**